Bringing Back Some Brightness

Brightness

20 Years of New Writing Scotland

(NEW WRITING SCOTLAND 22)

Edited by

VALERIE THORNTON
and
HAMISH WHYTE

with Maoilios Caimbeul (Gaelic Adviser)

Association for Scottish Literary Studies

Association for Scottish Literary Studies
c/o Department of Scottish History, 9 University Gardens
University of Glasgow, Glasgow G12 8QH
www.asls.org.uk

First published 2004

British Library Cataloguing in Publication Data

A CIP record for this book is available
from the British Library

ISBN 0–948877–60–X

The Association for Scottish Literary Studies
acknowledges the support of the Scottish Arts Council
towards the publication of this book

 Scottish
Arts Council

Typeset by Roger Booth Associates, Hassocks, West Sussex

Printed by Bell & Bain Ltd, Glasgow

CONTENTS

Hand	Alastair MacKie	9
The Vase	Jimmy Glen	10
Museum Piece	Hamish Whyte	12
Pilate At Fortingall	Edwin Morgan	13
Infertility Patient	Valerie Gillies	14
Voyeurism	Ian Rankin	15
Surrogate	Moira Burgess	23
Odd One Out	Roland Portchmouth	28
Three Poems From The Himalaya	Andrew Greig	29
The Dancing Hen	Gordon Meade	31
Portrait of a Shadow-Sailor	Ron Butlin	32
A Poem Containing The Word: Launderette	Gael Turnbull	34
Two Nights	Norman MacCaig	35
Fearless	Janice Galloway	36
Warm House	Graham Fulton	40
A Traditional Curse	John Glenday	41
Feet First	James McGonigal	42
A Fate Worse Than Ballet-Dancing	William Gilfedder	43
Glory Hole	Sandy Fenton	44
Dustie-Fute	David Kinloch	50
Boy	Robert Crawford	52
Joy	G.F. Dutton	53
The Day I Met The Queen Mother	John Herdman	54
The Flora And Fauna Of An Independent Scotland	Douglas Lipton	56
Huge Wobbling Bits of Chocolate	Jane Harris	59
Due	Janet Paisley	64
One Way	Marianne Carey	65
A Meditation Upon Penguins	A.L. Kennedy	66
Not About The Kids	Brian McCabe	70
All The Little Loved Ones	Dilys Rose	79
The Bridge	Iain Crichton Smith	84
Where The Debris Meets The Sea	Irvine Welsh	89

4

The Ghost of Liberace	John Maley	94
An Tuba	Dòmhnall Alasdair	95
The Drunken Lyricist	Gerry Cambridge	99
I Give Back Some Brightness	Robin Fulton	100
from: Peyps In My Diary	Brent Hodgson	101
As, As	Richard Price	105
Iain Grimble (1921-1995)	Derick Thomson	106
Nam Chlarsair Balbh	Rody Gorman	108
Nam Iain Odhar	Rody Gorman	109
Loch	Rody Gorman	110
Dubh	Rody Gorman	110
Dear Andrew McGregor	Donny O'Rourke	111
An Duibhre Beò	Aonghas MacNeacail	112
An Acarsaid	Kevin MacNeil	113
Leum Nam Buffalo	John Scott MacPherson	114
A Death in The Family	Pete Fortune	116
The Extra	Norman Kreitman	122
Air Tilleadh Dhachaigh	Meg Bateman	123
De Mortuis	David Cunningham	124
A Chitterin Bite	Anne Donovan	132
Interview with a Proddy Vampire	Paul Foy	140
Cave Canem	Rachel Yule	147
Kosovo	Stewart Conn	150
Eadar Àird A' Mhàsair is Ostaig	Murdo Stal MacDonald	153
This Shirt	Brian Whittingham	156
Speedy Delivery – Verbal Estimate	Margaret Beveridge	158
Dileab	Criosaidh Dick	159
René Magritte In Embro	James Robertson	164
Fish-Soup – A recipe	Ian Stephen	166
The Balemartin Bard	Jim Carruth	168
From: Synchronicities	Gerry Loose	169
Gilfedder	David S. Mackenzie	172
A Guide to Dumfries	Hugh McMillan	187
If Only Coll Were Two Floors Down	Valerie Thornton	188
Biographies		190

INTRODUCTION

I. Bringing Back Some Brightness

In the last twenty or so years *New Writing Scotland* has become a fixture on the Scottish literary scene. It is the only annual anthology publishing poetry, fiction and drama together, and in a country with limited publishing opportunities is a welcome outlet for writers. Its aim has always been to include both established writers as well as up-and-coming and even unknown ones – the emphasis being on new writing as opposed to new writers. (The name, by the way, was suggested by Alexander Scott, one of the first editors, with a nod towards the famous Penguin New Writing series.) *New Writing Scotland* has served, and we hope will continue to serve, as a useful annual report on what's happening in contemporary Scottish writing.

Twenty issues: 883 contributors (including many regulars) and nearly a thousand pieces of writing. Most of the famous names are there, from Norman MacCaig, Edwin Morgan, Naomi Mitchison, Iain Crichton Smith among the elders, to Iain Banks, Ian Rankin, A.L. Kennedy, Janice Galloway and Irvine Welsh of a more recent generation. It's a pretty good roll call and a matter of satisfaction that authors like Galloway, Kennedy and Welsh were early published in New Writing Scotland. And, of course, there are the one-offs, the fascinating eccentrics, the promising talents who just disappeared, as well as the Scotlit stalwarts who make up the bulk of the contents; the deliverers of regular good value.

Politically speaking, the first twenty issues of *New Writing Scotland* (1983-2002) cover roughly the years from no devolution to devolution (1978 referendum to 1999 parliament). Whether New Writing Scotland can be regarded as a kind of cultural barometer of these years is another question. What is perhaps clear is a lessening need on the part of Scottish writers to flaunt their Scottishness. A writer should, of course, be free to write about anything, but so many Scottish writers have in the past seemed to need to establish their national credentials. We do feel there is a confidence now in simply writing – about whatever.

In this selection from numbers 1-20 of *New Writing Scotland* there are perforce many stories and poems set in

Scotland or Scotland-related, but the guiding principle in choosing was the quality of the writing: the pieces that we felt were well written, that embodied an energy and an imaginative use of language, still stood up, were still fresh, had a confidence and an indefinable 'something' that made us want to read to the end.

There was so much to choose from and hard choices had to be made. A review of an early issue of New Writing Scotland compared it with a box of chocolates, some with soft centres, some with hard but most to everyone's taste. We hope this selection box provides some nourishment too, as well as giving the full flavour of New Writing Scotland of the past and acting as a taster for what's to come. Lastly, thanks to our fellow editors, who chose these pieces in the first place.

II. Looking Back over the Introductions

Twenty-one years ago, in November 1983, the very first New Writing Scotland arrived quietly, without even an introduction. It did, however, sport a bold blue thistle on the front cover.

By the following year it had become a target market for both new and established writers, and the high quality of submissions was a reassuring sign for the future of Scottish writing.

In 1985 there was a note of regret that no work in Gaelic and little in Scots was being submitted; an awareness that some of Scotland's story was not being told. Nonetheless, the editors, James Aitchison and Alexander Scott, were heartened by the 'refreshingly subversive vision' in the poetry.

As the size of New Writing Scotland expanded over the next few years, rising to 500 plus writers submitting several thousand manuscripts for consideration, the editors were pleased to note they could now include poetry in all three of the languages of Scotland. They also confirmed that the short story was a flourishing form in Scotland and that there was a diminishing and lamentable lack of outlets for writers in the country.

By 1987 the growth in writers' groups, even then, had become notable and the editors were sad to have to reject much excellent work from previous regulars because of lack of space. Although New Writing Scotland 5 included Scots prose, there was a 'melancholy forecast' for the future of Scots, which was perhaps instrumental in the consequent submission of a variety of Scots from newer writers. 'Lack of space' (for the amount of good writing being submitted) became a perennial lament and established writers began to lose out to new ones.

By *New Writing Scotland* 8 (1990), the first titled as opposed to numbered volume, there was also concern about lack of funding for future issues. Fortunately, the Association for Scottish Literary Studies decided the anthology was a valuable feature on the literary landscape and secured its position.

Since then *New Writing Scotland* has moved into the new millennium with one major change – all the submissions are now judged anonymously. This places the emphasis entirely on the quality of the work submitted. And still, there is not enough room for all the great writing sent to us.

Meanwhile the phenomenal rise of writers' workshops, and now even degree courses in creative writing, have assured healthy quantities of excellent new writing, much of which we hope will continue to come our way. Here's to the next twenty volumes, and beyond!

Valerie Thornton
Hamish Whyte
July 2004

NEW WRITING SCOTLAND 24

The twenty-fourth volume of *New Writing Scotland* will be published in summer 2006. Submissions are invited from writers resident in Scotland or Scots by birth or upbringing. Poetry, drama, short fiction or other creative prose may be submitted but not full-length plays or novels, though self-contained extracts are acceptable. The work must be neither previously published nor accepted for publication and may be in any of the languages of Scotland.

Submissions should be typed, double-spaced, on one side of the paper only and the sheets secured at the top-left corner. Prose pieces should carry an approximate word-count. **You should provide a covering letter, clearly marked with your name and address. Please do not put your name or other details on the individual works.** If you would like to receive an acknowledgement of receipt of your manuscript, please enclose a stamped addressed postcard. If you would like to be informed if your submission is unsuccessful, or if you would like your submissions returned, you should enclose a stamped addressed envelope with sufficient postage. Submissions should be sent by **30 September 2005**, in an A4 envelope marked for my attention, to the address below. We are sorry but we cannot accept submissions by fax or e-mail.

Please be aware that we have limited space in each edition, and therefore shorter pieces are more suitable – although longer items of exceptional quality may still be included. A maximum length of 3,500 words is suggested. Please send no more than two short stories and no more than six poems.

Duncan Jones
Managing Editor, *New Writing Scotland*
ASLS
c/o Department of Scottish History
9 University Gardens
University of Glasgow
Glasgow G12 8QH, Scotland
Tel: +44 (0)141 330 5309

Alastair MacKie   *1983*

HAND

It's a delta o functions,
aeons hae soopled.

And a map
runkled wi high roads.

A cleuk forby
I share wi the beasts.

And a barescrape
wi a skiftin o strae hair.

It has the face's weather,
its streetch o moods;

it can straik love
and thraw thrapples;

or be lowsed
in dreichness or soond sleep.

Its finger-nebs
snuff the skin o the world –

flooers, stane, wid, metal,
the things, oor neebors.

Brigs it maks
oot o handshaks.

Blinner than the een
it fichers in the dark

for the airt o things,
door-sneck or shouther-bane.

When the condies o the body
stop their pumpin

the hands lie on the breist
cuddling their tool bags.

Jimmy Glen   *1983*

THE VASE

I deliberately take a long time packing the rucksack. Had even taken out half of the clothes again so that my cassettes and tape recorder could lie amongst them to prevent damage. Toothbrush, paste and razor in the side pockets. Socks and pants. Asthma tablets (it had recurred during a recent holiday in Scarborough) and hay fever tablets (past the season but better to be safe). Thinking about the hair drier. No, I'll leave it for her though she'll probably never use it.

Derek should be arriving any moment in the Morris Traveller for a lift to the station, though he could be late. He usually is. The problem is whether to go through for a chat or just stay here. No point; just sit tight and wait for the horn.

My room was always dark, even on the brightest days, but today it seems dull beyond belief. The huge oak wardrobe sickens me utterly. I wanted rid of it for years and now it's rid of me. Funny. Wondering what the new room will be like. Probably very practical – yes, practical; chair, desk, bed, cupboard. That'll do fine.

Room C43, Tower block. Enough said.

I hear a noise outside and seconds later she calls from the other side of the door to tell me that Derek has arrived. I grab the rucksack and go quickly to the living room. Outside the window I can see the grass has been newly cut for the last time this year, the lawnmower still standing outside the hedge. Derek is sitting in the Morris on the other side of the road. The old man has just come in from the garden and he stands next to my grandmother to say goodbye. I reach out my hand, which he takes firmly, when his face breaks from the strain of keeping something in, and after hurriedly stuffing a fiver into my pocket, he walks quickly into the kitchen and out into the garden.

We move out into the hall and she hasn't said anything yet but her cheeks are wet and she seems somehow shrunken. I tower above her with one arm round her shoulder, the other dangling the rucksack inches off the floor. She tells me to take care son, and I tell her I will, I will, and I'll be back to see you once I've settled in and that but I can't cry. Not really. She is turning to open the front door when I hoist the rucksack clumsily onto my shoulder and it just catches the edge of the blue china vase which stands on top of the display cabinet. Her wedding gift. We both turn to watch it falling slowly through space to smash on the hard linoleum of the hallway, and whilst she cries out it doesn't matter son, it doesn't matter, I am already out the door and running towards the car.

As we are pulling away, I look round for one last time and I see the old man struggling to put the lawnmower into the garden shed and her face is at the window, staring.

Hamish Whyte   *1983*

MUSEUM PIECE

To the Art Galleries on a snow-threatened
Sunday afternoon; pushing into
the revolving doors, Kenneth and I: wee grey
duffel figure, bulky green coat shuffling behind.
I know he wants to see the dinosaurs,
the foxes (especially the one crunching a bird),
'The amours', even the pictures (to
recognise Degas's *Duranty* I have a postcard of –
'you've got that one' – I wish I had) –
but what I think he'd really like, is to go round and
round in the turning doors for ever
and ever, whirled without end.

Edwin Morgan   *1984*

PILATE AT FORTINGALL

A Latin harsh with Aramaicisms
poured from his lips incessantly; it made
no sense, for surely he was mad. The glade
of birches shamed his rags, in paroxysms
he stumbled, toga'd, furred, blear, brittle, grey.
They told us he sat there beneath the yew
even in downpours; ate dog-scraps. Crows flew
from prehistoric stone to stone all day.
'See him now.' He crawled to the cattle-trough
at dusk, jumbled the water still it sloshed
and spilled into the hoof-mush in blue strands,
slapped with useless despair each sodden cuff,
and washed his hands, and watched his hands, and washed
his hands, and watched his hands, and washed his hands.

Published in *Collected Poems*, Edwin Morgan
(Carcanet, 1990). Reproduced by permission.

Valerie Gillies   *1985*

INFERTILITY PATIENT

'I could never have enough children.' Katherine Mansfield

To lift another woman's child
is like carrying a bundle of barbed wire.
And one who will let himself be held
stirs every bereaved desire.

Between collarbone and breast
his hard head makes an impression:
a dent in a white quilt
someone's secretly been sleeping on.

My hands fall empty in my lap
when she lifts him away.
I can share, as I give him up,
only his backwards look with no wave.

She's the fertile one while I am not.
Inject a dye and see my tubes are drawn
blocked and scarred, death's first print I've got
in me: you month, rat's jaw, I see you yawn.

Ian Rankin

VOYEURISM

A crisp October day it was when the nun fell from the sky and landed at his feet. He had been sitting all morning in the small, badly-lit office, listening to the telephone answering machine's messages of the night before. He gripped a pencil in his left hand, though there were few names and addresses to be noted. He knew the rules of the game well enough by now not to expect anything else. Soon he tired of hearing the ritual: telephone rings, activates machine, Jill the secretary's voice.

'Hello there.' (Coy, sexy. The reality was oh so different: forty-five, bovine, married to a brute of a coalminer.) 'If you've phoned this umber then you must have seen one of our advertisements in your local newspaper. We are J & J Videos Limited, a family-run concern whose aim is to bring you the very best in uncensored adult videos.'

And so on, even featuring a few seconds' recording of some grunting from one of 'our select choice'. Then:

'If you would like to receive our catalogue, absolutely free and with no commitment, sent discreetly under plain cover, then simply leave your name and address when you hear the bleep. I look forward to dealing with you soon. Bye-bye now.'

Then: bleep, a pause, total silence, the line goes dead. The man on the other end has had his cheap thrill, but hasn't the guts to speak into a machine, hasn't the guts to reveal his identity.

That happens often. Out of seventeen calls he gets five names and addresses: three from the Midlands, one from Glasgow, one from London. On two occasions a name has been half-uttered before the shaky voice has packed in and put down the receiver. He smirks at those, rewinds them and listens again.

So, five potential customers for whom he must write out five envelopes, fold and push a cheaply reproduced catalogue into each, stick down and post. Then home for his lunch. What a job. He looks around the back office, the walls of which are resplendent with faded pictures of old football players torn out of boys' magazines. Ironical that. On a table sits an unsteady pile of videos in their sleeves. 'Hot Stuffing', 'Geisha Frolics', 'Wild Vixen Party 2'. He smirks again at the dreadful titles. When he had first started the job, the real perk had been to slot one of these video cassettes into the recorder, sitting back to view the wares.

But no longer a perk. Sometimes friends or associates will want to spend the afternoon in the back office watching a skin flick. When they do, face wrinkles with anticipated boredom, tiredness in his fingers as he pushes home the desired cassette. His boss, too, is tired of the whole thing. For him, the tapes are merchandise to be distributed, the money collected and put into the bank, a wife and two sons at home with the evening meal before him and normal lives to be lived. To him, the tapes are Christmas toys, slabs of butcher-meat, supermarket-shelf biscuits. They used to be other, but that was long ago.

By twelve, he has licked shut the last of the sour envelopes and has taped them all for further security. He shoves them into a polythene bag, locks up the office, locks the shop and whistles in the crisp air of another October lunch-hour. Sometimes he really does feel alive, as when the birds hop reassuringly towards him to receive their scraps of park-bench leftovers. At times like that he forgets that he is dirty, smutty, lewd. He feels just the same as everyone around him. They too, after all, have their secret lives and tentative lusts. They are the people who would respond to a telephone number in a newspaper, safe in their anonymity, but would not deign to leave their name and address. They were despicable in their anonymity. At least he was open about his work. He had even told his mother once, discreetly, over the phone. She had not appeared to understand, and he had left it at that. All she seemed able to comprehend was that he was involved in film and TV distribution. Had he met any of the actors? No, mother, he had not. Nor would wish to.

A crisp October day, as stated, it was when the nun dropped from the sky and landed at his very feet on a quiet path on his way home.

'In the name of Christ!' he shouted, startled. The nun was startled also.

She looked at him for a second, her mouth open, before turning on her heels and trotting off along the pavement. He wiped his hand across his forehead, examining the high wall which ran the length of the pavement. She had jumped from this wall, behind which lay the convent of the Sisters of the Sacred Heart, its glazed and bolted wooden doors standing thirty yards further up the street. He looked again at the top of the wall. It took guts to jump from a wall that high. Then it struck him: she had nearly killed him. Had she landed on top of him, and he decided a moment earlier to sprint home, he would have been flattened beneath her billowing robes. He tingled at the thought and looked along the pavement to where the nun was disappearing around the far corner. His mind made up, he began his sprint.

It took him all of a minute to catch up with her, and even then he could not bring himself to use a hand or an arm to halt her, for he was not sure whether nuns were allowed to be touched and he thought that probably they weren't. So he walked along beside the nun, trying to catch her eye, while she pointedly ignored him and walked quickly along the crackling paving stones.

'Miss, eh, Sister. Hold on there a minute. You nearly killed me back there. Nearly gave me a heart attack you did. Hold on.'

She stopped and drew breath. Her cheeks were strawberry coloured, not all with the effort of running, and her eyes were brown like a young animal's.

'Sorry,' she said. She began to walk on. He caught her up again.

'It isn't every day I encounter nuns falling from the skies, you know. What's it all about?'

'Swimming,' she said, not stopping, not looking at him.

'Swimming?'

'Though I can't for the life of me think why I'm telling you.'

'Swimming?'

'It's got nothing to do with you really. Nothing at all. Now if you'll excuse me,' and with that she began to cross the road.

'Swimming?' he called from where he stood.

She stopped in the middle of the deserted street.

'Swimming,' she said. 'Swimming, yes, swimming, swimming, swimming.'

'Alright,' he said, approaching her and wondering what she looked like beneath the thick material of her habit, 'keep your hair on. What colour *is* your hair as a matter of interest, professional interest you understand?'

She turned away and began to walk. He walked beside her.

'Professional interest?' she said at last.

'I'm a toupee maker,' he said.

'I don't believe that.'

'And how do you expect me to believe that swimming has anything to do with leaping commando-style from a ruddy great wall?'

'I am about to go swimming. It is my weakness, may the Lord forgive me. I come out of the convent twice a month and go swimming.'

'At the local baths?'

She did not answer.

'You like swimming?'

'It is the only thing I miss, living in the convent.'

'How long have you been inside?'

'You make it sound like prison.'

'Isn't it?'

'Certainly not. It is the very opposite. It is a liberating experience.'

He nodded, agreeably, he hoped, and she saw him nodding and smiled just a fraction.

'You're pretty when you smile.'

She stopped smiling.

'Where's your swimming costume then?'

'At a friend's.'

'That's where you're off to just now is it?'

'Go away.'

'Okay. Goodbye, Sister.' And with that he went, but not far. He walked around the corner and waited a minute. He heard her shoes clack on the cobbles, then stop, checking that he was not following, then start to move again at a brisk pace. At that, he put his head around the corner. She was at the end of the short street, turning into the doorway of one of the tenements. Her friend's house, he presumed, thinking himself clever.

That afternoon, back at the office and dealing with any orders that came through, he toyed with his pencil and thought of the lucky nun. She was lucky because she had her secret life, her little thrill (there was no other, more modest way of putting it). Perhaps technically she was sinning by leaving her convent, perhaps she would burn in Hell for it, because she believed in Hell. She had been tempted by the thought of a public baths, and she had fallen. She was lucky. Life still held for her the fortnightly promise of an unjaded, vicarious pleasure. For him there was no such hope. He slotted a cassette into the recorder, turned on the television, and fast-forwarded through another romp. It was all over in less than nine minutes. He felt numb, his eyes glazed like the rainwater on that cobbled street. He thought of his nun and her swimming.

He counted out the days as if he were a child again and this his Advent. After much thought, on the ordained day he took the afternoon off and went to the baths. Not to swim, no, for his body was a mockery to him; just to watch. He paid his money and climbed the dull stairway to the spectator's gallery. A woman was up there, waving down to her children who splashed and did brave manoeuvres in order to impress her. He sat close to this woman at the very front of the balcony. And looked down. Mostly children. They screeched, and their screeches bounced off the steamy glass roof, echoing around the pool. They played and got water in their eyes and cried.

As he had once cried.

There was a couple of teenage boys as well, who walked around the edge of the pool and studied a clutch of teenage girls, three of them, who were bobbing in a ring in the centre of the water. He studied these girls, watched as one of them kicked away from her friends and swam, her legs snapping like crocodile-grips, to the edge of the pool. She eased herself out of the pool and, pulling at the costume, sat at the side of the water on the warm tiles. He watched her intently through the rising wisps of steam. Blobs of eyeliner highlighted the red rims of her eyes. She pulled the hair back from her face and kicked water at her friends. The boys hovered near her, unable to make the telling move, though the girl's friends giggled encouragingly from their retreat.

He became so entangled in this burgeoning romance that he failed to notice, for some time, the elegant underwater motion of the perfect swimmer, the body at ease in its airless environment, the head arched back, eyes wide on the approaching wall, then somersault, breath, kick and away again, a half-length before another breath was necessary.

But, as the head came up again for its gulp of salty air, he caught the face, and his gaze turned away from the antics of the girls and boys. His nun was pushing her way slowly and without apparent effort through the water, teasing it, assuring it of its lifeless quality. This was not the splashing and stinging water of the children, nor was it the bobbing water of the girls and their desires. It was silent water, a thing to be used, a willing pet to the cutting strokes of its mistress. And she moved as though she owned it, and had trained it well. And he watched her, holding his own breath, releasing it whenever she rose out of the ripples to breathe again. He wondered what she was thinking. She looked as if her total concentration was focussed upon the act itself, nothing more, and he followed her as if she were a large and admired fish which stayed always just out of reach of his line. Slowly he became less tense. He sat deeper back into the hard wooden seat and enjoyed the performance. The slow motion. The playback.

After thirty or forty lengths she rested her shoulders against the wall at the deep end and bobbed a little, moving her feet and with her arms languid along the edges of the tiles. And it was then, as she cleared the water away from her face, that she saw him. She looked away, then looked back. Her eyes closed a little, and her mouth opened as if to suck in liquid through a straw. She gazed down on the surface of the water, which reflected his distorted image, stretching him out as on a rack. Then she kicked towards the steps and left the pool quickly.

He watched her as she glided on tiptoe towards and into the changing area. From his position he could see a tiny portion of the interior. Little girls scampered about on their toes, splashing the dregs of water around them. But his nun stayed invisible, as though she had slipped behind a mirror.

When she left the baths, not without apprehension, she was dressed in a simple frock and belted coat, a carrier-bag slung over one arm, but when she left her friend's flat twenty minutes later, she was dressed in her habit, and her whole gait had changed perceptibly: her arms now angled from the elbows, rather than retaining the straight, flowing motion they had when she left the baths, and her feet were placed flat on the pavement, their purpose unshakeable. He followed her all the way back to the convent, intrigued by everything, and watched as she tapped on a small side door and was allowed inside, doubtless by another willing accomplice.

He waited out his two weeks and returned to the poolside, dressed in his swimming-trunks this time and looking pale and unathletic beside the children. He blushed when some water stung him in the eyes, kicked up by an angelic monster who smiled up at her mother in the watchful gallery. He waded into the surprisingly cold water (surprising for the amount of steam rising from it) and did his imitation of a doggie paddle. After half a length he grew tired, his lungs pushing outward as if frantic for release from his rib-cage, and he half-walked to the side of the pool, resting, gripping the edge with his fingers, blowing hard.

Gooseflesh settled on him, and he dipped often beneath the water. After thirty minutes of this he knew that he had scared her away. The girls were there, and their boyfriends, grappling with one another in the water until the attendant blew his whistle and signalled for them to keep their distance. Quite right, and in a public baths too. He climbed heavily out of the water and trotted to his cubicle.

A fortnight after that he went again, as a spectator this time. There was no sign of her. He reasoned that she had changed her day for coming. For a solid week of afternoons he sat it out, the woman at the kiosk frowning suspiciously at him. She knew his sort, and he knew it was useless to reason with her. When she asked him one final day what his game was, he stopped going to the baths altogether.

He gnawed at himself inwardly, arguing his need to see her again. He wanted to apologise for having spied on her, wanted to tell her how much he admired her, and how much he envied her passion for swimming. But he had spoiled all that, hadn't he? She did not allow herself to go swimming now. He had put a stop to that, to her only pleasure. He needed her forgiveness; that was the truth of it. He needed to tell her about his job, about his feelings, about the way he had been nullified by it all, by what he did and what he was forced into becoming and what he had made of himself. He needed to tell someone other than himself. He chewed his pencil, listening to a morning batch of answering-machine messages and growing sick in his heart. He grew sick as he listened to click after click, as he listened to all the anonymous callers becoming afraid and deciding in a flurry of panic to remain anonymous. Even worse in a way, he listened to those who confidently gave their name and address, awaiting the sordid merchandise. One of them even said a cheery 'Thank you' before putting down the receiver. One – one of the anonymous – was abusive. He weakened, feeling his mind and his stomach churning in unison, switched off the machine, and went for a walk.

No nuns fell from the sky, but he had an idea during his stroll amongst the children and the dogs of the local common. He returned to the office and reached into the drawer for the telephone directory. He would ask if he could leave a message for her. It did not matter that he did not know her name. He would say an old friend with whom he swam regularly had joined the Order and could he speak to her please now that he was back in the country. He found the number and, his heart beating as though he were fifteen again and arranging his first date, dialled the convent.

The phone rang once and once only. That was quick. He began to speak but was interrupted.

'Hello, this is The Sisters of the Sacred Heart. Please leave your message after the signal. God bless you.'

The electronic bleep.

He opened his mouth again. An answering machine! He listened as the machine whirred, the tape running. He licked his lips. He couldn't speak to an answering machine! It was ridiculous. He tried to formulate some message, but nothing would come. His fingers trembled. Shocked, frightened, finally numbed, he slammed down the telephone, thumping on it with his fist.

'Damn you,' he said. 'Damn you, damn you, damn you.'

But in his heart of hearts he was hoping for the reverse.

Moira Burgess   *1985*

SURROGATE

'There's someone,' the old woman said, 'who knows exactly what I do and when I do it.'

I was surprised at the way she burst out with it, since of course she didn't know me at all. The two young pregnant mothers ahead of us, with whom we'd been idly discussing the headlines, had just been called, one to each surgery. Now we were alone in the waiting-room; I suppose I was reassuringly on her side of forty, and perhaps even had a good-listener look. She was quite agitated, her shiny knotted hands with the dark liver-spots folding and refolding the tabloid in her lap. 'Cathie, 83, Mugged', the blaring letters spelled.

'What do you mean?' I said, looking concerned. I was really rather interested to hear what she'd say.

For such an old bag of bones she was concise enough. 'There are notes,' she said, 'messages. Always when I'm out. The police won't do anything. They just say it must have been a friend. I tell them there isn't anybody left who would be calling, but I think they think I'm a bit forgetful. I'm seventy-nine, you see.'

'Oh, that's no age,' I said with a smile. 'My mother's over eighty and everybody says she's good for her century.'

'That's nice,' said Miss Jenner in an abstracted way. (I pulled myself up for even thinking of her as Miss Jenner. It wouldn't do if I used her name, when she hadn't given it to me.) 'They're not rude or anything, you know.'

'The police?'

'The notes,' she said a little testily. 'They say, oh, things like *Sorry I missed you*. Or *Will call back*. That worried me for a whole week. And once, *Hope you enjoyed the concert*.'

Her faded eyes held mine as if anyone ought to see the horror of that. I put on a puzzled look.

'I'd *been* at a concert,' she whined. 'Don't you see? How did they know?'

'You must have mentioned it,' I said, 'in a shop, or – or at the bus stop or something.'

'But that means they were standing near me.' Her old hands weren't at all steady. 'Listening... I'm almost afraid to open my mouth now.'

You don't say, I thought sarcastically. I said in my mother-soothing voice, 'I wouldn't worry. I'm sure there's nothing in it. You don't get phone-calls, do you?'

'Yes!' she cried, certainly shaking now. 'They never speak. I answer, and the phone goes down. It's got so that I tremble for an hour. I'd have the phone taken out, but I really need it. I have angina, you know.'

'So has my mother,' I said. 'It's a very crippling condition, isn't it?'

'Well, it needn't be,' said Miss Jenner with unexpected spirit. 'If you take your pills and behave sensibly, that is.'

'My mother's must be very bad. She can hardly do anything for herself.'

'Are you sure it's angina?'

'No,' I said, 'but she is.' That had slipped out: there was an unwelcome dawning in her pale-blue eyes. Time to tip the balance a little. 'What I wonder about those phone-calls, if I were you,' I said, frowning, 'is how the person knows your number.'

'I wonder that too,' she gasped. I thought she was in for an attack right there in the waiting-room. 'I've wondered and wondered –'

'Perhaps a tradesman you've had in?' But apparently she hadn't had even a plumber for years. I could imagine her basement flat, damp-furred wallpaper, crumbling sills. 'The meter-reader? The minister?'

'*The minister?*' That really gave her something to think about: I was afraid I had gone a little too far. But she was a loyal Presbyterian. 'No, no. But my name's on my pension book ... And I suppose the chemist knows it ... And there's the voter's roll, they could look up the phone-book from that –'

'You might have been carrying a case with a label on it,' I suggested, 'when you were going on holiday some time.'

That rang a bell. 'Last summer,' she said. 'I'd been ill, and I went to a little convalescent home on the coast. Yes, I remember, I did put a label on my bag. In case it went astray, you know.' She gazed at me, blaming herself, her fingers splayed on her thin old chest. You could almost see the palpitations. 'They must have been on the train! Beside me!'

'Or in the bus shelter,' I said innocently, which of course was how it had been.

Fortunately just then the pregnant ladies emerged almost together from the two surgeries, and in a moment the two doctors' lights blinked on.

'I see Dr Fraser,' I said, getting up. 'Look after yourself now, Miss – ?'

'Miss Jenner, Emma Jenner,' said the old idiot, now in such a state that she really didn't know she was telling me.

'Emma,' I said smiling, 'What a pretty name. My mother's name is Emily, strangely enough.'

I was in the surgery with the door closed before she had tottered half-way across the floor. Her doctor would get an earful today. I settled myself for a chat with Dr Fraser, but I'm sorry to say I didn't get the attention I deserved.

'You're in very good shape for your age, Marina.' Dr Fraser had known me from babyhood and irritatingly still used my flowery and dated first name. When mother died and I moved into a flat of my own, I would call myself Jane. 'What you're describing are tension signs. Do you get enough exercise?'

'I take Mother for her walk in the park every day.'

'How do you sleep?'

'All right, I suppose.' Except that I was constantly in a half-doze in case Mother should call. Just twice in twenty years she had called when I was too sound asleep to hear. 'Marina would sleep through the last trump,' she sweetly informed every friend who came to tea.

Dr Fraser leaned back in his chair and took off his glasses. 'How is your mother?' he said.

'She doesn't seem to keep very well.'

'She hasn't been in to see me, has she? Do you want to make an appointment for her?'

'I don't think she could get to the surgery, doctor.'

'Marina, you pass by here on your way to the park.'

I came out with that argument unresolved and a prescription for more tranquillisers. I thought I could hear Miss Jenner's breathy little voice from the second surgery. Worth hanging about in the chemist's, you never knew what you might learn; and sure enough she came fluttering along in a few minutes with a prescription in her tiny claw. We laughed and exclaimed at meeting up again so soon.

'More pills,' she apologised.

'Mine shouldn't be long.' It would be nearly as long as hers, since I'd handed it over the counter as I saw her cross the road from the doctor's. 'I'm just looking for a hot-water bottle while I wait.'

Choosing that, and belatedly remembering toothpaste, kept me in the shop until Miss Jenner was stowing her bottle of pills in her handbag. We came out together into the windy, fresh spring day. Long ago at university I had joined the hill-walking club. I had stood on the tops three or four times, seeing the quilted mountains stretch north and west. Then Mother had found out, and the idea of me in such danger had brought on her first heart-attack. Today I wouldn't stand on a hilltop in the cold sweet breeze. I would go home to our too-big, musty house, and Mother would complain that I'd been away a long time.

'Which way do you go, Miss Jenner?'

'Up to Thornhill, dear. It's not far away, only I have to take it slowly nowadays.'

'I'm just over the hill. Do let me carry your shopping-bag.'

'That's really kind of you, dear.'

We toiled up the hill. 'Marina, is that you? You've been nearly an hour! Where have you been?' Miss Jenner's patient bent head bobbed away below my shoulder, blue felt hat, neat-ly rolled white hair. 'I don't think you realise, Marina, what it's like for me sitting here alone. What if the phone should ring? What if somebody tried the door?' My flat, when she died, would be on the crest of a hill, fronting the westerly breeze. 'Please shut that window, Marina. You know about my back.'

Miss Jenner, panting, asked humbly if she might stop for a rest. 'You seemed to be walking a little more quickly there, dear.' I stopped. The fresh breeze felt calm. I stood in the dull heavy street with an old woman, as always, by my side.

'Here we are, dear.'

There wasn't a soul to be seen in the peeling terrace of bed-sitter houses. The other side of the street was a run-down play-park with dogs' dirt trampled into the shabby grass. I carried her shopping-bag down the basement steps and stood like a dutiful daughter while her uncertain fingers turned three keys. I leaned forward to put the bag inside the door. There were four more steps, rather steep, leading down into the greasy little kitchen with its old green gas cooker and its stone sink.

'Thank you so much, dear,' said Miss Jenner, setting her shaky foot on the top step. 'Perhaps I'll see you again.'

'Perhaps,' I said.

It only took one push, and as her head struck the corner of the sink there was one hard thud. People would take it for the slamming of a car door. 'Goodbye now,' I cheerfully said. I closed the door firmly so that the lock clicked, and went back home to Mother.

Roland Portchmouth

ODD ONE OUT

No one in our family has ever been famous for anything
outside the family. Inside the family though, and among
   ourselves
there's more than one with quite a reputation
– the sort bought by Sunday newspapers and much admired
by amateur psychologists. Several of us would be well-known
   cases
if someone in the family had split on the rest;
but none of us has, tending rather
to dry up when things start leaking out. After all,
we run to largish numbers, and in any crowd
there's bound to be the homely lunatic or public nuisance,
the shameful and the shameless, the one with a flowery vest
under the pin-stripe suit, or a plastic apron
beneath the ocelot fur coat. There's always
the meek, retired gas fitter inflamed to insane vengeance
by one greenfly on his rose bush; and the bison-chested
   builder
who reads Pixie Frolics to his six infants after work
affecting all the different falsetto voices; and the pale antique
   lady
who accosts a diesel truck with rake and rancour
for stopping at her garden gate emitting dense fumes.
There's no doubt about it – a family as big as ours
hasn't a chance of being normal. Turn an uncle
and you'll find an auntie no one knew about; turn auntie
and you'll surprise three old railwaymen we always thought
left the district to improve themselves. Largely on account
of being a close family, we keep in touch and have no secrets
– which is probably the reason the less particular
invent a few.
               And that's the point:
               some quite distorted facts
have circulated recently it seems, and the time has come
for one of us to act responsibly. Because of this,
I'm disclaiming now any connection with it.

Andrew Greig   *1987*

THREE POEMS FROM THE HIMALAYA

1 Desire

Between one expedition and the next
we buried the tiny Buddha's bones
upright, with respect, at the bottom of the garden.

We were driven
back to the mountains
on the crumbling verge of tears.

Between the highway and the ditch,
thirled to desire, the restless West
is pushing to its limits –

no one said we are too old
to die young, too young to retire
as we left Lhasa behind.

2 Arrival

We're back again
with our tents, our trash
and more. Be arrogant:
we animate these mountains.

(Whether a stone does or does not
fall when we're not here
is a toy metaphysic
fiddled in spare moments
like headtorches or letters from home.)

Mal flicks his lighter
and an avalanche roars into life –
we have come to assert
everything fits
that it might do so.
This is the true scale of things:
the entire mountain mirrored in our shades.

All day snow sank in the billy,
was boiled, drunk, peed, replenished
as we passed the mountain through us.
Night came on, meaning something
in the presence of witnesses.
Unblinking stars and lightning,
the darkness is lit
at a depth we can rely on.

3 Interlude on Mustagh Tower

In these high places we are melting out
of all that made us rigid; our ice-screws
hang loose on the fixed ropes to the Col.
Monday in the Himalaya. The clouds are down,
our objective is somewhere but obscure,
let it soar without us for a day.
We lounge in thermals on the glacier,
brewing and shooting the breeze, the improbable
project of conversation between the living.
Our laughter rings across the ice. Why not?
None of us will die today, that's immortality
you can taste and pull on in a cigarette,
sweet and rasping, the way we like it.
Steam rises from the billy, Sandy pours;
it is true high, worked for, that we pass
hand to hand between us with our brews.
Men on ice, going nowhere and laughing
at everything we cannot see but know
is there – in the cloud, on the Col,
a hand of some sort is tightening our screws.

Gordon Meade   *1987*

THE DANCING HEN

I remember Jimmy Duncan
And his way with animals.
How he loved to show us
His dancing hens.

How it meant him holding
Them by the neck, while
He rendered them feminine
With a pair of rusty

Pliers. How his hens
Would dance, and sing.

And I remember Netty Duncan,
How she'd walk for miles
To find the right tree,
To chop down. How one day,

her electric saw slipped
Her hold, and danced along
her thigh. How she walked
Three miles back to the farm,

Her hand held tight against
A severed artery, the saw
Tucked underneath her arm.

Ron Butlin *1987*

PORTRAIT OF A SHADOW-SAILOR

At thirty-five years old
he's halfway round his lifetime's only world
– quite at sea. (*That*, at least, is true).
By day he plays the captain and the crew
whose rank and medals have been tattooed on
– gentle pinpricks cutting to the bone.
At night he lies and listens: the crow's nest sways
almost audibly above, and weighs
out silence for the darkened scene below
– letting the slightest measure only, flow
into his sea-crazed mind.

Tightening his grip upon the helm
(in 'lock-position') the shadow-sailor calms
approaching storms by will-power. He reshapes
the cliffs and waves according to his maps;
their tears and creases mean what he decides
in terms of shallows, hidden reefs. He prides
himself upon a life's experience
of reading charts long out of date: he glides
across the wind-scarred surface, making sense
of every ocean-contour (this one hides
a bogeyman within its childish scrawls,
and that one traps a god). Such reverence!
In these deserted sea-lanes he collides
with ghost-ships – their slow and soundless passage falls
shadowless across his decks and hull.

Sea-wraiths and the demons who preside
upon the ocean-floor advise him; coral
(saturated with the sudden cries
of drowning men) signifies their power.
These are his familiars; their histories
are his; their voices he alone can hear;
their silence is the elemental measure
of despair.

Thus his world has taken shape:
a place of terror, clashing rocks, the hiss
of cross-run currents, undertows to rip
his soul apart ...

His log's kept neat for he believes that this
– i.e. the mastery of words, and clear
calligraphy – improves the truth. His fear,
therefore, must complement the sentence-structure
or be dropped. Each entry's much the same;
new page, top left: 'The heat, the chill, the heaving
sea beneath are everything I know
– yet sometimes I an sense a tide whose flow
runs greater, and carries to a farther shore.
Too briefly, then, I glimpse and recognise
what lies beyond this shadow-sea, these shadow skies ...'

As evening falls he watches ocean-colours
and the sun dissolve into each other
letting their transparency reveal
the night sky and the ocean-floor:

The heavens' slow creation and destruction
the shadow sailor takes into himself,
letting constellations drift at random:

– until he's made, of stars and minerals,
the darkness his imagination spills
unearthly light upon.

Gael Turnbull   *1987*

A POEM CONTAINING THE WORD: LAUNDERETTE

containing the word: launderette
the words: finest equipment
the words: oily overalls, horse tack and muddy sports
    gear you must not, repeat underlined must not
    attempt to wash, in these machines
the words: load drum, amount detergent, add appropriate,
    desired wash, select cycle, coin in slot, proper
    amount, push slide, fabric softener, add before
    'rinse light' ON, again after 'rinse light' OFF,
    not complete until 'lid light' OUT, will not open
    until 'lid locked light' is also
then by pressing the words (it distinctly says
    'pressing the words') 'High' 'Low' 'Permanent Press'
    as required, ensure you follow in sequence the words
    to pre-set the dryer, then by pressing the word
    'Start' and re-pressing if need be
compressing, expressing, rinsing and cleaning,
    refreshing and drying, restarting, resetting
in a word, with words: a launderette, containing a
    poem

Norman MacCaig   *1987*

TWO NIGHTS

The real night, the one
that keeps coming back on time,
never begins
with a gash of black.

As though, politely,
it makes a noise on the gravel
and coughs and knocks at the door
before coming in.

Not like the other one, that
on the most summer of days
gashes the light and pours through
a black dark with no moon, no stars.

'Two Nights' from *Collected Poems* by Norman MacCaig
published by Chatto & Windus. Used by permission of the
Random House Group.

Janice Galloway   *1988*

FEARLESS

There would be days when you didn't see him and then days
when you did. He just appeared suddenly, shouting threats up
the main street then went away again. You didn't question it.
Nobody said anything to Fearless. You just averted your eyes
when he was there and laughed about him when he wasn't.
Behind his back. It was what you did.

Fearless was a very wee man in a greasy gaberdine coat meant
for a much bigger specimen altogether. Greygreen sleeves
dripped over permanent fists so just a row of yellow knuckles,
like stained teeth, showed below the cuffs. One of these fisted
hands carried a black, waxed canvas bag with an inept burst up
one seam. He had a gammy leg as well, so every second step,
the bag clinked, a noise like a rusty tap, regular as a heartbeat.
    He wore a deceptively cheery bunnet like Paw Broon's over
an escape of raw, red neck that hinted a crewcut underneath,
but that would've meant he went to the barber's on a regular
basis, keeping his hair so short, and sat in like everybody else
waiting his turn, so it was hard to credit and since you never
saw him without the bunnet you never knew for sure. And he
had these terrible specs. Thick as the bottoms of milk bottles,
one lens patched with elastoplast. Sometimes his eyes looked
crossed through these terrible specs but it was hard to be sure
because you didn't get to look long enough to see. Fearless
wouldn't let you.

There was a general assumption he was a tramp. A lot of people
called him a tramp because he always wore the same clothes and
he was filthy but he wasn't a tramp. He had his own house down
the shore front scheme; big black finger-stains round the keyhole
and the curtains always shut. You could see him sometimes,
scrabbling at the door to get in, looking suspiciously over his
shoulder while he was forcing the key to fit. There were usually
dirty plates on the doorstep too. The old woman next door
cooked his meals and laid them on the step because he wouldn't
answer the door. He sometimes took them and he sometimes
didn't. Depended on his mood. Either way, there were usually
dirty plates. The council cut his grass, he had daffodils for christ-

sake – he wasn't a tramp. He was the kind that got tramps a bad name: dirty, foulmouthed, violent and drunk. He was an alkie all right, but not a tramp: the two don't necessarily follow.

The thing about Fearless was that he lived in a state of permanent anger. And the thing he was angriest about was being looked at. Sometimes he called it MAKING A FOOL OF and nobody was allowed to get away with it. It was a rule and he had to spend a lot of time making sure everybody knew it. He would storm up and down the main street, threatening, checking every face just in case they didn't know, then if he thought he'd caught you looking he would stop, stiffen and shout WHO ARE YOU TRYING TO MAKE A FOOL OF and attack. Sometimes he just attacked: depending on his mood. Your part was to work out what sort of mood it was and try to adjust to it, make the allowance. It was what you were supposed to do. Most folk obliged, too – went out of their way to avoid his maybe-squinty eyes or pointedly NOT LOOK when they heard the clink and drag, clink and drag, like Marley's ghost, coming up the street. Then the air would fall ominously silent while he stopped, checking out a suspicious back, reinforcing his law. On a bad day, he would just attack anyway to be on the safe side. Just in case. You couldn't afford to get too secure. There was even a story about a mongrel stray he'd wound into a half-nelson because it didn't drop its gaze quick enough, but that was probably just a story. Funnier than the catalogue of petty scraps, blows that sometimes connected and sometimes didn't that made up the truth. It might have been true right enough but that wasn't the point. The point was you were supposed to laugh. You were meant to think he was funny. Fearless: the very name raised smiles and humorous expectations. Women shouted their weans in at night with HERE'S FEARLESS COMING, or squashed tantrums with the warning YOU'LL END UP LIKE FEARLESS. Weans made caricatures with hunchback shoulders, cross-eyes and a limp. Like Richard the Third. A bogeyman. And men? I have to be careful here. I belonged to the world of women and children on two counts, so I never had access to their private thoughts voiced in private places: the bookie's, the barber's, the pub. Maybe they said things in there I can have no conception of. Some may have thought he was a poor old soul who had gone to the bad after his wife left him. Romantics. I suppose there were some who could afford to be. Or maybe they saw him as an embarrassment, a misfit, a joke. I don't know. What I do know is that I never saw any of them shut him up when the anger started or try and calm it down. I remember what women did: leaving food on the doorstep and bottles for him to get money on; I remember women shaking their heads as he went past and keeping their eyes and their children low. But I don't remember any men doing anything much at all. He didn't seem to touch their lives in the same way. They let him get on with what he did as his business. There was a kind of respect for what he was, almost as if he had a right to hurl his fists, spit, eff and blind – christ, some people seemed to admire this drunken wee tragedy as a local hero. They called him *a character. Fearless is a character right enough* they would say and smile, a smile that accounted for boys being boys or something like that. Even polismen did it. And women who wanted to be thought above the herd – one of the boys.

After all, you had to remember his wife had left him. It was our fault really. So we had to put up with it the way we put up with everything else that didn't make sense or wasn't fair; the hard, volatile maleness of the whole West Coast Legend. You felt it would have been shameful, disloyal even, to admit you hated and feared it. So you kept quiet and turned your eyes away.

It's hard to find the words for this even now. I certainly had none then, when I was wee and Fearless was still alive and rampaging. I would keek out at him from behind my mother's coat, watching him limp and clink up the main street and not understand. He made me sick with fear and anger. I didn't understand why he was let to fill the street with himself and his swearing. I didn't understand why people ignored him. Till one day the back he chose to stop and stare at was my mother's.

We were standing facing a shopwindow, her hand in mine, thick through two layers of winter gloves. The shopwindow was full of fireplaces. And Fearless was coming up the street. I could see him from the other end of the street, closer and closer, clinking the black bag and wheeling at irregular intervals seeing if he could catch somebody looking. The shouting was getting louder while we stood, looking in at these fireplaces. It's unlikely she was actually interested in fireplaces: she was just doing what she was supposed to do in the hope he'd leave us alone – and teaching me to do the same, I suppose. Fearless got closer. Then

I saw his reflection in the glass: three days' growth, the bunnet, the taped-up specs. He had jerked round, right behind where we were standing and stopped. He looked at our backs for a long time, face contorted with indecision. What on earth did he think we were plotting, a woman and a wean in a pixie hat? What was it that threatened? But something did and he stared and stared, making us bide his time. I was hot and cold at once, suddenly sick because I knew it was our turn, our day for Fearless. I closed my eyes. And it started. A lot of loud, jaggy words came out the black hole of his mouth. I didn't know the meanings but I felt their pressure. I knew they were bad. And I knew they were aimed at my mother. I turned slowly and looked: a reflex of outrage beyond my control. I was staring at him with my face blazing and I couldn't stop. Then I saw he was staring back with these pebble-glass eyes. The words had stopped. And I realised I was looking at Fearless.

There was a long second of panic, then something else did the thinking for me. All I saw was a flash of white sock with my foot attached, swinging out and battering into his shin. It must have hurt me more than it hurt him but I'm not all that clear on the details. The whole thing did not finish as heroically as I'd have liked. I remember Fearless limping away, clutching the ankle with his free hand and shouting about a liberty, and my mother shaking the living daylights out of me, a furious telling off, and a warning I'd be found dead, strangled up a close one day and never to do anything like that again.

It was all a long time ago. My mother is dead, and so, surely, is Fearless. But I still hear something like him; the chink and drag from the closemouth in the dark, coming across open, derelict spaces at night, blustering at bus-stops where I have to wait alone. With every other woman, though we're still slow to admit it, I hear it, still trying to lay down the rules. It's more insistent now because we're less ready to comply, look away and know our place. And I still see men smiling and ignoring it because they don't give a damn. They don't need to. It's not their battle. But it was ours and it still is. I hear my mother too and the warning is never far away. But I never could take a telling.

The outrage is still strong, and I kick like a mule.

Graham Fulton   *1988*

WARM HOUSING

Morning bleach,
a smoky silence
    ribboning heaven,
and moon
    reluctant to
leave the sky.
Humans.
Over the wall
    with the wire on top
the empty homes
    are being refurbished, primed
for the reflux
    of Council tenants.
November.
    Sweat-men,
by daylight, stroll
    on the slates, scratch
at the plasters
    and look
in the sparkling bathroom;
    the wild
winter yards
    by night are host
to warm shapes
    of drinking boys
building fires and works of fire,
    out of control.
Powder-pyramids, rockets, rockets.
    Remember.
Remember,
    the bloody wire
keeps nothing out.
    Shards of life, sound,
sight, a symphony
    of starlit stupors
and bottles
    becoming broken bottles.

John Glenday   *1988*

A TRADITIONAL CURSE

When apoplexy
strikes, may you
not die.

May you revive
beneath a calm sky,
hanging larks,

freshly stamped turf.
May you retain
the breath to cry out

strongly, tasting
stale air
which dribbles

from your box
like colourless
sand.

And may somebody
lingering close by
hear you. The fool

whose village you burned,
picking earth
from his nails.

James McGonigal   *1988*

FEET FIRST

Babies, we first said hello to ourselves
shaking hands with our feet.
Five little nipples to nuzzle

to little avail. Years later we shoved them
in grey woollen sacks,
endless kittens for drowning.

They lost their looks early. The onus
of bearing our load
left them plain and hard hearted

yet they never failed to organise
a trip from A to B, each
in their duty overtaking the other.

After many a tight corner
nightfall released them
into dreams of warm water.

Now in cool morning air they stretch
out on the covers
after lying till dawn in each other's arms.

Old age will stagger them,
younger limbs
carry them home to the dark.

William Gilfedder   *1988*

A FATE WORSE THAN BALLET-DANCING

One can just imagine the scene
Father takes son aside
Whit dae ye want tae be when ye leave school son
A poet daddy
Crack, away and don't be so illiterate
Nae son a mines is gonni dangle words for a living
Could ye no dae something a bit mer manly
Like live off the immoral earnings of a prostitute
Theres nothing cissy in that
And if ye mention that word poetry in this hoose again
I'll take ye oot the back
And kick the living fear of God intae yi
Until the offending material
And whoever it wis put ye up to this
Have been well and holy exorcised.
But daddy whit if its intuitive?
Then in that case son we'll get you a private tutor.

Sandy Fenton   *1989*

GLORY HOLE

Gweed kens fa pit it in – ah weel, no, gweed kens an' I ken, an'
it wisna me, bit gin I tellt ye, some een mith get tae hear o't, an'
syne 'ere'd be ower mony maisters, as 'e taid said till 'e harra.
Weel, there wis nae dogs an' nae cats aboot 'e hoose, an' nae
ither kin's o' beas' tae ait it, an' ye couldna mak' porrich or
brose wi't – nae unless ye wis ready tae pick caff oot o' yer
chowdlers for 'e rest o' 'e day. I niver speert far it cam fae, bit
intill 'e glory hole it geed, a plastic baggie o' bran that mith ay
'a' come in handy for something.

If 'id been 'ere a lang time. A glory hole's nae a place ye min'
tae keep snod. If ye're needin' something oot o' 'e road, in it
goes, an' gey lucky if ony reddin up's deen eence a 'ear. Files I've
gotten scunnert masel an' I've teen oot 'e ironin' byeurd, siveral
pairs o' sheen, boxes 'it hid been teemt bit niver trampit on an'
tied up for 'e scaffie, newspapers – God! newspapers,
Scotsmans, wik-eyn Observers, a fyow aal Sunday Times, a
pucklie People's Journals and People's Freen's 'at hid got wach-
let doon fae 'e Northeast, Sunday Expresses 'at 'e dother brocht
roon fin she cam for 'er Sunday denner an' didna ay min' tae tak
awa again, colour supplements, wifies' papers 'at tellt ye aa
aboot Charles an' Diane an' geed ye yer horoscope as weel's 'e
latest cure for breist cancer, nae tae spik o' heapies o' cut-oot re-
sipes an' squaars o' faalt-oot sweetie papers an' choclit wrap-
pins' – tinnies o' pint an' a baldie-heidit brush 'at no't a new
wig, teem biscuit tins 'at some o' 'e trock kidda been stappit
intil, twa coal shovels in 'perfect condeetion' as 'ey say in 'e
adverts, twa or three great big boxes o' Ariel washin' pooder,
een o' 'em half skailt ower 'e bit o' aal linoleum 'at didna richt
cover 'e fleer, fire irons on a cowpit imitation brass stand o' best
weddin' present quality, a plastic pyock full o' plastic pyocks,
an', aye, bit 'e best bittie o' aa, 'at wis 'e nyeuk I'd teen ower
masel. I'd gotten haad o' a timmer box, pat dowel rods until't,
up an' doon an' across, an' made a fine rackie for 'e wine I bocht
be 'e dizzen bottles fae ma freen Roddy, gettin' a bittie off for
bulk buyin'. I likit 'e fite wines mair'n 'e reed, bit nae aabody his
'e same tastes so I ay tried tae cater for ither fowk tee.

Ah, weel, eence aathing wis oot 'ere wis a kinna teem stewy
smell – funny, doon by here 'e fowk wid say 'stoory', or raither

'stooray' – bit I niver likit tae spile 'e wye I wis brocht up tae spik. I ken 'e wird 'stoory' fine bit ye winna get me sayin't. An' I winna say, 'It'll no dae' fin I've aye said 'it winna dee'. 'E queer bittie o't is, it's ither wyes o' spikkin in ma ain country I'd raither nae folla, though I scutter on fine wi' ither fowks' languages. Even aifter gettin' in 'e lang spoot o' 'e Hoover, ye'd ay get that stewy kinna atmosphere, so naething for't bit tae pit aathing back in again, or maistly aathing.

Though I used 'e glory hole for ma wine cellar it wisna a' that caal. Een o' yon nicht-storage heaters wis in 'e passage aside 'e glory-hole door, though of coorse ye daardna turn't on in the summer. It wis bad enyeuch in 'e winter files makin' sure 'e heat wis on. Niver min' 'at, though, it's nae winter I'm spikkin aboot.

Eence 'e warmer days cam – 'is wis last 'ear – an' ye could keep 'e back door open, I noticet a lot o' little beasties comin' in. Fin 'e licht geed on at nicht, 'ey'd bizz aboot it. Haad awa fae 'e bluebottles, though, naebody peyed attention till 'em. Noo 'an aan ye'd get a bite 'at raised an' reedened 'e skin, bit 'ere wisna much o' that. It's jist aboot 'e eyn o' 'e simmer 'at ye daarna gang till 'e heid o' 'e gairden for fear o' gettin' bitten. If ye pick a flooer or twa, or hae a hagger at 'e hedge, neesht mornin' yer cweets'll be aa up, gey sair, an' yer wrists, like enyeuch yer back an', warst o' aa, in anaith 'e oxters. Fit ondeemous beasts 'is is ye canna ken 'cos ye canna see 'em, though there m'n be a lot aboot. Onywey, they're amon' 'e girse an' 'e flooers an' 'e leaves o' 'e beech-hedge, an' they bide there as lang as they're nae disturbit. I dinna even like tae cut 'e green at 'at time. Fin I div, nae tae be black-affrontit be 'e length o' the foggage, there's nae question bit fit it'll be intill 'e eyntment tin afore bedtime.

There cam a time fin I noticet 'ere wis an aafa lot o' moths aboot 'e hoose. In 'e extension at 'e back, far 'ey cam in fae oot-side, 'ere wis 'e odd mothie, sma' eens wi' licht broon wings. They took a fyow turns aboot 'e place, got a bit o' a scaam on 'e electric licht bulbs, an' syne they jist disappeared. I wisna botheret aboot 'e-em. Bit in e wall o' 'e stair, 'ere wis fit lookit like anither breed athegither. Ye'd notice em on 'e curtains o' 'e stair-windae, an' on 'e wa', an' on 'e grey-pintit widden uprichts o' 'e bannister, an' some got intill 'e dinin'-room, an' 'e rooms up 'e stair. I happent tae mention 'is moths, an' oh, they were jist normal for 'is time 'o 'ear. I didna jist agree, but ye never won be conterin'; aa 'e same, a fyow days later 'e plastic baggie wis haaled oot o' 'e glory hole. 'E plastic wis holet in a curn places, an' 'ere wis nae doot it hid been a great hame for God kens foo mony maivs amon' 'e bran, as lang's bran wis. But fit she took oot wis naething bit sids, as I saa fin I cairried it up till 'e heid o' 'e gairden, an' haavert 'e pyock wi' ma knife tae let 'e birds an' only ither hungry craiters get at fit wis left. Ye ken, it lay for days an' naething touched it Ye'd a thocht there was something queer aboot it. It was 'e rain an' 'e win' in 'e eyn at did awa wi't, an' maybe it wis' o' some eese for muck, though fit wi' 'e big sycamore in ae nyeuk an' a haathorn in 'e idder, there wisna air an' licht eneuch for much in 'e wye o' vegetables, an' fither the kitchie-gairden bit got muckit or no made little odds.

Noo, 'is moths fae 'e brodmel in 'e glory hole wis big. They hid lang kinna bodies, an' a rich, dark broon colour 'at fairly gart em stan' oot on a licht wa. For a start 'ere wisna aa that mony, an' though I k-nackit 'e odd een or two an 'e wye up till 'e bathroom – they ay cam oot fin it wis jist comin' on tae gloamin'– I thocht little aboot it for a fyle.

In 'e middle o' 'is, I got a fortnicht tae look aifter 'e place be masel, a job I ay likit, though I hid tae min' tae keep tee wi' fool socks an' sarks an' hankies, bit 'at didna hinner lang. I ay managed tae mak mait tae masel aa richt tee, an' I could get vrocht awa at ma bitties o' writin' withoot 'e television dirlin' in may lug. I aften sat lang intil 'e evenin' wi' 'e back door open, lettin' e air blaa aboot 'e place, an' listenin' till 'e chirps an' fustles o' the birds as 'ey sattled doon for 'e nicht. Be 'is time 'e cats 'at stravaigit aboot hid geen inside, nae forgettin' 'e rent-a-cat 'at aften cam tae sleep in 'e hoose, an' syne held on its roons. Gweed kens far it cam fae, bit it wis weel fed, an' a freen'ly breet, an' it wis ay a bit o' company if ye no't that. It's a fine kinna time, 'e gloamin'.

Ay fin I geet up 'e stair 'ere wis mair moths. I began tae keep 'e kitchie door shut tae haad 'em oot o' 'e sittin' room. Fin I pit on 'e passage licht, I'd look aroon an' spot 'e broon shapies. At first it wisna sae hard taw connach 'em wi' the pint o' ma finger, an' fin I'd cleared 'e stair as far as I c'd judge, I'd hae a scan room 'e spare room an' ma ain bedroom. Half-a-dizzen wis a low coont, an' een though 'e baggie 'at bred and maitit 'em wis gone, they seemed tae hae an aafa pooer o' appearin'. Fit wis mair, ye'd a thocht they kent 'ere wis something gettin' at 'em, for aifter a fyow nichts they didna bide still in 'e wye o' moths, bit gin ye made a move they'd be up an' awa. A lot o' 'em got in till 'e heich bit o' 'e ceilin', oot o' ma reach. I took an aal'

paper, faalt it intill a cudgel an' let lick at 'em wi' 'at. Still there
wis mair farrer up, an' I'd tae start haivin' 'e paper abeen ma
heid fae a step on 'e stair tee till 'e riggin, an' files I got een an'
files I didna. I'd finish up pechin', an' aifter half-a-dizzen close
misses ye'd fairly get yer dander up an' start at 'em withoot
takin' richt time tae aim, an' at's nae ma usual wye o' workin'.
Anither queer thing: ony ye knockit aff 'eir perch wi' 'e win' o'
'e paper wid wheel, wheel aboot yer heid, till ye begood tae be
confoondit, an' ye'd start haadin' yer breath for fear o' sookin'
een in. It didna maitter foo hard ye tried tae keep yer e'e on 'em
tae see far they'd licht, 'ey meeved 'at quick an' quairt ye'd seen
loase 'em.

    'Is geed on for a lot o' nichts. Fin ye wis oot o' 'e hoose be
day ye'd think o' 'em in 'e stair-wall, an' tryin' tae settle 'e question, I bocht some packets o' Mothaks an' sprayed 'em aboot
'e hoose, hingin' 'em up amon' claes, drappin' 'em in ahin
byeuks, layin' 'em on shelves an' peltin' a hanfae intae the glory
hole itself till ye'd 'a thocht aa livin' beas' wid 'a smoored. Did
it mak a difference? Did it hell. The moths dreeve on as afore,
an' I doot they startit tae spread mair aboot 'e hoose, for I got
a fyow in 'e dinin'-room.

    Aifter a file I wis thinkin' aboot 'em near aa 'e time. I geed
roon ilky room mair'n twice a nicht, feelin' ay mair like 'e
Kommandant o' 'e prison-camp at Belsen as I poppit een, syne
anither against 'e wa'. I wid dream aboot 'em. The first thing I
did in 'e mornin' wis tae see if I could spy oot ony o' 'e buggers,
afore I scrapit ma phisog an' geed masel a gweed dicht doon wi'
saip an' watter as I ay dee. I'd shak ma claes tae see if ony
moths fell oot o' 'em. I'd heist e' valance o' 'e bed – weel, it
wisna a valance exactly, jist a cover 'at hung doon a' roon – tae
see there wis neen there. At ma wirk in 'e office, or at meetin's,
nae maitter foo I wis catchet up in maitters o' ootstandin'
importance (for 'e meenitie, onywey), ony dark spot aboot e'
place wid draa ma e'en an' 'e thocht o' moths wid flit throwe
ma heid like 'e eident stabbin' o' a coorse conscience. An' hame
I'd gang an' intae 'e slachter again.

    I widda shut ma bedroom door, bit a wa'-tae-wa' carpet hid
been laid, an' ye'd a deen damage tryin' tae reemish 'e door tee,
an' mair haalin't open again, so I jist left it open a crackie. It's
fine tae streek yersel oot on yer bed if ye've been scoorin' on aa
day, an' 'is nicht I wis glaid tae lie doon an' steek ma e'en,
though nae without a hinmist look aroon for only o' 'at naisty

broon craiters. Nae sign o' onything. Aa richt, let 'e inhibition so' 'e day slip, forget aboot 'is 'ferocious work ethic' 'at Northeast bodies is blamet for haein', even if 'ey wirk in 'e sooth, stop thinkin', dream a bittie aboot yer freen's, an' aff ye go tae sleep.

Aye, I did. Bit I wisna athegither easy. There wis a droll kinna feelin' in 'e air, an' though I'd seen nae moths they werena aa 'at far oot o' ma thochts. Ye ken 'at queer 'eemir a body gets intill files, fin 'e kinna slips oot o' 'e clay mool', an' floats aboot lookin' doom at 'imsel', hooseless in a wye, bit tied tae the bleed an' muscle an' been tee? Weel, 'at wis 'e wye o't 'at nicht. I c'd see 'e room fine, an' 'e bed, an' me on't. An' throwe 'e crack in 'e door cam a fyow broon bodies, they begood tae swarm like bees, ay mair comin' in, an' niver a soon' fae only o' 'em, keepin' in a ticht, roon' ba', maybe nae aa 'at ticht for ye c'd see throwe't, bit still it wis a gey solid like collection.

I'm een o' 'is fowk 'at likes tae start sleepin' flat on their stamach, ae airm stracht doon, 'e ither at an angle, an' ma nieve half steekit aside ma chin. Though I start 'at wye, I've aye noticet 'at be mornin', I'm ower clean 'e conter road, flat on ma back, wi' ma han's up tae ma kist like a corp waiting fir 'e trump tae soon'. As lang's I wis on ma face, the moths jist hoveret, 'e hale birn swayin' back an' fore a bit, bit 'ere wisna a lot o' meevement, at least neen ye could jist see, though their wings ma'n 'a' been wafflin up an' doon jist eneuch tae haad 'em floatin'. I meeved fae 'e richt tae 'e left side, swappin airms, bit 'e pilla wis a bittie heich or aan 'e cover wis lirkit, I dinna ken fit, it wisna richt comfortable, sae I furled roon wi' ma face oot abeen 'e blankets, took a deep breath or twa, syne sattled doon again.

Noo 'e swarm cam tae life. It drifted ower jist abeen ma face. For aa 'at ye'd ken, it startit tae split up, till ye c'd see two sma' pucklies an' a big een. They come hoverin' ower's an' as I breathed oot they raise a bittie, an' as I breathed in they cam a bittie closer, like a balloon balanced on 'e tap 'o an updracht. 'Is geed on for a wee fylie. Syne, in 'is aafa quairtness, ma mou' opent a bit as a sleepin' man's mou' dis. Wi' 'at, 'e moths meeved. The two sma' pucklies geed for ma nose, an' the bigger een for ma mou', a kinna cheenge o' a glory hole. Some stray eens geed on fleein', back an' fore. I shut ma mou', bit 'e moths were in. I sookit air throwe ma nose, bit hit wis blockit, an' drawin' in blockit it mair. I tried tae hoast, bit ma throat wis steekit an' fecht as I likit nae breath c'd I get. In a meenit or twa ma nieves lowsent. Ma een hid niver opent an' they niver wid. The fyow moths left hoveret a meenitie mair, syne vanished fae sicht. Fae the bed, there wis nae movement. Fae the left-han' wick o' ma mou' cam a thin trail o' broon stuff, like 'e slivers at ran doon e' chin o' aal Hatton at hame, fin 'e cam tae help ma fadder tae brak muck, aye cha-chaain' at 'eez tebacca, an' 'ere wis a sprinklin' o' darker specks tee.

Fin I wakent 'e neesht mornin', there wis a weet spot aside ma heid on 'e pilla. Bit there wis nae sign o' moths aifter 'at, it wis jist a clean toon. A lot o' months later, I wis kirnin amon' cardboord boxes an' books in een o' 'e rooms, knockin' aff stew, an giein some files o' paperies a dunt on 'e fleer. Fit fell oot o' een bit a moth-grub, fite wi' a black neb, an' 'e biggest I've ivver seen. 'Ere's an aafa books an' papers aboot 'e hoose. An' aa this wa'-tae-wa' carpets, ye canna see fit's in anaith. An' 'e glory hole's as fu' as ivver it wis, an' 'e smell o' Mothaks his worn aff. I'm nae lookin forrit tae simmer.

David Kinloch   *1989*

DUSTIE-FUTE

When I opened my window and reached for the yoghurt cool-
ing on the outside ledge, it had gone. All that remained was a
single Scottish word bewildered by the Paris winter frost and the
lights of its riverbank motorways. What can 'dustie-fute' have
to say to a night like this? How can it dangle on its hyphen
down into the rue Geoffroy L'Asnier where Danton stayed on
the eve of revolution? How can it tame this strangeness for me
or change me into the strange cupolas and flagstones I so desire
yet still notice everytime I walk on them? Does the 'auld
alliance' of words and things stand a chance among the traffic
and pimps in the Publicis Saint-Germain? These are the wrong
questions. For it's not as if 'dustie-fute' was my familiar, not as
if it could float down like soft gauze and make the city sneeze so
that I could wake up tomorrow and be able to say bless-you to
its snow-covered streets. I could easily confuse 'dustie-fute' with
'elfmill' which is the sound made by a worm in the timber of a
house, supposed by the vulgar to be preternatural. This is also
called the 'chackie-mill'. These words are as foreign as the city
they have parachuted into, dead words slipping on the sill of a
living metropolis. They are extremes that touch like dangerous
wires and the only hope for them, for us, is the space they
inhabit, a room Cioran speaks of, veering between dilettantism
and dynamite. Old Scots word, big French city and, in between,
abysmal me: ane merchand or creamer, quha hes na certain
dwelling place, quhair the dust may be dicht fra his feete or
schone. Dustie-fute, a stranger, equivalent to fairandman at a
loss in the empty soul of his ancestors' beautiful language and in
the soulless city of his compeers who are living the twenty-first
century now and scoff at his medieval wares. And here, precisely
here, is their rendezvous and triumphantly, stuffed down his
sock, an oblique sense, the dustie-fute of 'revelry', the acrobat,
the juggler who accompanies the toe-belled jongleur with his
merchant's comic fairground face. He reaches deep into his base
latinity, into his pede-pulverosi from which his French descen-
dants pull their own pieds poudreux. Dustie-fute remembers
previous lives amid the plate glass of Les Halles. They magnify
his motley, his midi-oranges, his hawker lyrics and for a second
Beaubourg words graze Scottish glass then glance apart. In this

revelry differences copulate, become more visible and bearable and, stranger than the words or city I inhabit, I reach for my yoghurt and find it there.

Robert Crawford   *1990*

BOY

My left hand is turning into a herring.
The fingers I write with get doughy

So it hurts to shake hands – feel as if
People tear at my fingers like rolls.

I want to greet them with my left. They shun it
Because it has a briny smell,

But out here is a strange place I'm learning
To cope with offering both hands

To the sitting crowd. When they grip me, each man and woman
Seems full. This

Must be the meaning of shaking hands
With five thousand people. They're rising,

Fed, leaving the bowl of the hills
Strewn with left-overs, me among them.

Everybody's gone now. I'm just thirteen.
I understand I don't understand it.

'Boy' from *Talkies* by Robert Crawford published by Chatto
and Windus. Used by permission of The Ramdom House
Group.

G.F. Dutton   *1990*

JOY

Twenty-seven bullfinches
in one week
of sun

visited the blossom –
so sparse
now the years

close in – of his cherry trees
from Japan. They enjoyed
each opening bud

as much as he did, not
for the whiteness
not for food

but for the delight
of ripping them out
and throwing them down, a circle of white

blenching the grass
under each tree. Pure
anarchy, sheer

destruction. There was something about them
misusing the sun
for private joy

that offended his sense
of our common inheritance. And must have been why
each day, he shot them.

Twenty-seven bullfinches
in one week of sun. The best,
almost, with that particular gun.

'Joy' from *The Bare Abundance* by **G.F. Dutton** published
by **Bloodaxe Books. Used by permission of the publisher.**

John Herdman   *1990*

THE DAY I MET THE QUEEN MOTHER

That day started just like any other day. I got up, washed, had
my breakfast, caught the bus to work. How could I possibly
have known that before I got back into bed that night, I would
have met the Queen Mother?

The lower deck of the bus was full up as usual, so I climbed
upstairs and established myself on one of the seats at the front
end which are designated as a No-Smoking area. We had not
travelled the distance of one stop when a man sitting in front of
me, wearing a great big flowery hat, took a packet of cigarettes
from his pocket and lit up! I tapped him lightly on the shoulder,
and when he turned round I pointed wordlessly at the No-
Smoking sign on the window beside him. He turned away and
continued smoking for about half a minute in order not to lose
face; then he dropped his cigarette on the floor, stubbed it out
with his toe and left his seat, remarking as he went, 'I think I'll
go somewhere where the company is pleasanter.'

'Who in the name of God was that?' I asked a decent,
sensible-looking, middle-aged woman sitting across from me,
for I was surprised by his attitude.

'That's the Queen Mother,' she replied.

You could have knocked me over with a feather! That was
not what I thought the Queen Mother was like at all – either in
manners or appearance! In the first place the man looked about
forty-three, whereas the Queen Mother is an old thing of about
ninety. Then he might well have been a queen, uncapitalised,
but a mother, even lower-case, scarcely! Unlike the QM, again,
he had a long, angular, grey face, and was dressed in a scruffy,
grubby, stained anorak. Indeed the only thing he had in common with the said gracious lady was his enormous flowery hat.

It occurred to me, therefore, that my informant might be
insane, and had concluded merely from the fact that the man
was wearing a big flowery hat, that he must be the Queen
Mother. It is a well-known failing of the insane to take a mere
adjunct or accident as a defining characteristic. In my childhood I learned from my mother that our lunatic asylums are
filled with mentally disturbed persons who can be divided into
two principal categories: those labouring under the impression
that they are Napoleon, and those, seated on pieces of toast,

who believe themselves to be poached eggs. For our present purposes the first category is irrelevant and can be forgotten. But what an extraordinary thing, I always felt, to conclude simply from the fact that one happened to be sitting on a piece of toast, that one must be a poached egg! After all, compared to a poached egg, a human being is very large in relation to the average slice of toast. And again, many other things can rest on a piece of toast – baked beans, for instance, or tinned spaghetti, to name but two! However, many mentally sick people are also deficient in imagination.

But wait, I hear you protest, are you not overlooking something? May it not be you, who ask, that these people do not believe themselves to be poached eggs merely because they happen to find themselves sitting on a slice of toast, but, on the contrary, they sit on toast because they believe themselves to be poached eggs? And you are right, for it was this objection precisely that now occurred to me! And, applying this insight to the case of the Queen Mother, we would have to conclude that it was more likely to be the man in the hat than the sensible-looking woman who was insane; because, although the latter might have insanely concluded, from the fact that the man was wearing the hat, that he was the Queen Mother, the obverse deduction – that because he was the Queen Mother he must therefore be wearing the hat – cannot, in her case, be made meaningful. But if we assume the *man* to be insane, the conclusion is very different. What more unlikely than that he should assume, merely because he was wearing a big flowery hat, that he was the Queen Mother? – for many other people, besides the said gracious lady, though admittedly less famous, wear big flowery hats. If, on the other hand, he already believed himself to be the Queen Mother, what could be more natural – more inevitable, one might even say – than that he should, to enforce, as it were, the identity, don just such a headgear?

Yes, but… granted that the man could be insane, was it likely that such a decent and sensible-looking woman would simply have taken him at his word on such a dubious claim? Sometimes I almost wonder if I may not be going a little crazy myself – could I just have imagined it all?!! No, but seriously… if you are really looking for something to give me for my birthday (although, as I keep saying, I really don't want *anything*), I can think of nothing I'd like more than *The Bumper Book of Queen Elizabeth the Queen Mother.*

Douglas Lipton   *1990*

from: THE FLORA AND FAUNA OF AN
INDEPENDENT SCOTLAND

Dunnock

Aye, aye. Aw right. But at least
Ah'm no' a speug – scruffy wee nyaffs.

Midge

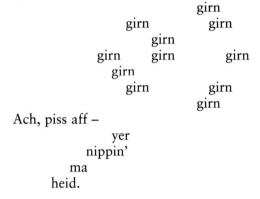

Ach, piss aff –
              yer
          nippin'
      ma
    heid.

Hedgehog

Yin fur the road, eh?

Scots Pine

Aye, D'they no' jeest.

Grouse

Wouldn't you, wi' Sir Mildly-Truffled's
gun up yir numph?

Spider

Yin mair go fur luck, eh?
D'ye fancy yir chaunces this time?

Great Auk

Whae's like us? –
Damned few,
an'
we're
aw
deid.

White-Tailed Sea Eagle

Aye, Ah'm jist back
furra wee luik. Scotland's
biggest burd o' prey, Ah wus.
Nevir mind they Gowden Eagles
an' Ospreys; Ah'm the boay.
Wha daur meddle wi' me, eh?
Ah'll mebbe see ye.

Hooded Crow

Corbies, ya bass!
Raptors is thick as mince.

Rabbit

Whit's the yin maist important
legacy o' the Norman Conquest
north o' the Border?
AH AM.
– Rabbit the Bruce.
An' yir mixie cannae stop me noo.
Ooops!

Buzzard

Shut yir geggie.
An' here's yin fur yir fud.

Red Deer

Bonnie Scotland's favourite
sex-symbol, me. Yir National
pin-up boay. But Ah ken fine
the price o' fame.
Ye'll be comin' tae ma perty, tho'?
Aye, it's fancy-dress aw right.

Otter

Playfu' otter? Aye, that's me
aw right. Jist luve a bit o' fun
an' a wee laff wi' ma mates.
As lang as there's nane o'
your lot aroond tae see.

Shag

Awa an' fuck yersel'.

Highland Cattle

Gie's a break. D'ye think
Ah like it here – oxter deep
in glaur an' ma heid fizzin'
wi' midgies? An' ye ken whit
ye can dae wi' thon camera.

Jane Harris

HUGE WOBBLING BITS OF CHOCOLATE

First thing I realise this morning is I need fresh air so I crawl off the sofa-bed without disturbing Philip yeah. Though it'd serve him right, the bugger. The larger the man the louder the snore that's my experience. Looks like mine hosts are still asleep too, so I sneak outside. Delightful house. Super people. Shame I got stomach-ache and couldn't eat dinner. Mind you, dear Philip compensated for my lack of appetite. Not half.

Okay I find one of those shops that sell everything from detergent to Puff Candy and I buy some Auntie Flo's Tablet Cups. Seem to have developed a sweet tooth in my dotage. Have a walk a suck and a think. I detest this town. Yes, it's got a castle and some galleries but where's its soul, that's what I always say to people. I said that to Lynn last night. Don't think she was best pleased. The atmosphere was a little sour at times yeah. Maybe because we're working in the same theatre. On top of each other. Yes.

Anyway once I'm pos they're all awake I head for la maison. Philip is sitting in the living room with his back to the window, reading *The Times Literary*. Oh apt apt. I tap on the glass and would you believe, he closes the paper, folds it, places it on the floor, stands up, turns round and nods at me. Very decisively. As if he wasn't certain who might be scraping at the window. Who else does he suppose it'd be you know, and why didn't he just look over his shoulder? God.

Dear Philip. He's so methodical it drives me absolutely barmy. Once, he was stuffing taco shells with salad yeah, one little ribbon of lettuce at a time. But the lettuce didn't fit quite the way he wanted, so he'd tease it out and prod it in again. I just stood beside him at the worktop. Watching. For, ooh about 15 minutes. Of course there are other times, maybe when he's been particularly witty or clever, that I look at him and think: one could do a lot worse. Indeed, one has done. More often than one cares to remember dear.

After a bit more nodding he realises I want to come in. Not bad for a MENSA member ay? He opens the door, then scuttles back into the living room and hides behind the paper. Lynn's in the kitchen making coffee, thank heaven. Her husband Dave is holding one of those multi-cereals, the ones where you get eight small packs you know each with a different kind of cereal in yeah. He looks absolutely astonished. Staring at the little boxes and shaking his head. 'I don't know if I can face these,' he says. He has a Dublin accent so everything he says sounds terribly caustic and thrilling.

'Have an egg then,' says Lynn.

'An egg,' says Dave. 'Would you like an egg, Robert?' he says to me with a glint in his eye, like a man suggesting we embark on a wonderful adventure together.

'No thanks. Just coffee,' I say. A quick coffee, big hugs all round, then leave. Pronto. Disappear. Philip can go to his bloody exhibition or whatever and I can shoot off home. You know what it's like, people stay overnight and in the morning they want fed again and they're under your feet and you think: God's teeth, when are they going to leave yeah?

'What about Philip? Would he like an egg?' asks Dave.

'I shouldn't think so,' I say. I smile. We're all standing very close together because their kitchen is quite small. 'You could ask him.' I only add this because I'm damn sure Phil will want to trot off to a gallery.

I follow Dave to the living room and can't help noticing how well made the dear boy is. I walk in, to hear him repeating after Philip: 'Some cereal, orange juice, a soft-boiled egg, not too soft, some toast and a pot of tea? That's right?'

'That's right. That will be lovely,' says Philip. Dave slides past me, muttering Philip's order.

Well. I sit on the couch and stare into my cup. We shall be here for days. This is really de trop. Philip hoists his paper and folds it mercilessly. One would think we were strangers in a hotel lobby. He is being particularly irritating lately. If I didn't know it would look bad, I'd walk out now. Alone.

Lynn arrives with the cereals. She shows them to Philip.

'Which cereal would you like Philip?' she says. She's so polite. If I were her I'd cuff him across the face with the box.

'Ooh,' says Philip, grabbing it from her. 'Let me see.'

'Just pour the lot into one bowl,' I say. This is me taking a swipe at Philip's weight problem yeah. 'Crack an egg in. Marvellous for his coat.'

Philip laughs good and hard at that one. Hig hig hig. His cheeks are pink and delighted. They meet his shoulders with no apparent pause for jaw or neck.

'Cornflakes would be lovely,' he says, handing Lynn the

cereal box like it's a menu. I have to keep reminding myself not to clench my teeth.

Lynn fetches a metal tray. On it is a jug, a glass of orange juice and a bowl.

'Here you are Phil. Sit up,' Lynn says. She should have stuck to bloody nursing and left arts admin untainted.

Philip discards the *Times Lit*, rearranges his buttocks in the seat, evacuates his throat, swallows, then allows her to place the tray on his knees. No wonder I forget he's only in his thirties; there are times when he acts older than me.

'Okay,' says Lynn sunnily to nobody in particular, and goes back to the kitchen. I select a book and try to read but I'm somehow compelled to keep an eye on dear Phil. Call it morbid fascination.

First he takes the jug and pours a good helping of milk into the bowl. Not too much so that it's swimming. Just enough to cover the flakes. Next, he slides the spoon in there, getting the amount he wants, exactly. Drains off some milk. So it won't drip on the shirt front dear. Keeping his head very still, he raises the spoon and pokes cereal into his mouth. Then he chews. One is instantly reminded of the sound of jackboots, marching on autumn leaves. I don't suppose he can help the noise really. After all, they are cornflakes.

As he eats, he gazes straight ahead through his specs; he could be watching his own reflection in a mirror. There's a dreamy look in his eyes. I often imagine him like this before we met, sedating himself with rice pudding and god knows what in that dreadful bedsit. He swallows, then shunts his spoon into the cereal and repeats the process. Until his bowl is empty.

One slug, and the juice is gone. He raises four podgy fingers to his mouth, puffs a couple of belches at them, and waits for someone to clear away his dishes.

Right on cue.

'Everything OK?' Lynn asks.

'Smashing thanks,' he says. 'Yeah.' He nods his head about seven times and purses his lips seriously, like he's thinking really hard about how smashing the cornflakes were.

'Good,' says Lynn. She takes the tray. 'More coffee Robert?' she asks.

'Yes please,' I say. 'I'll come and get it myself.' I glance at Philip to see if he noticed this last remark, but he's attempting, with a great deal of rustling and gasping, to tame *The Observer.*

Dave and Lynn are having breakfast in the kitchen. They're listening to the Archers. I pour coffee and tell them how super the book I'm reading is. I assure them we'll be off in two shakes. No problem they say. So sweet. I stroll back to the couch in the lounge. There seems to be nowhere else to go.

As I drink my coffee, I find I'm remembering when I was a student. Funny how the mind wanders. A group of us were in my friend Caroline's house. We were smoking. Talking. Caroline and her boyfriend Iain weren't getting on, they were pretty much at the end of the relationship by then. We were all eating sweets and this tiny piece of chocolate lodged in the corner of Caroline's mouth. She hadn't noticed yeah but Iain did. He was an American. I'll never forget him glaring at her with his lip curled, saying:

'Jesus Caroline. You've got huge wobbling bits of chocolate all over your face.'

But there was just this one little crumb. God. Not long after that they split up.

Hurrah! here's dear Lynn with a boiled egg, some margarine, a plate, a knife, everything he'll ever need for a cup of tea, and a teaspoon.

'There you go Philip,' she says. She sounds as if she's about to burst out laughing any second. But doesn't. Philip casts his paper aside, clucks till his arse is comfy, then accepts the tray.

'I'll bring your toast through in a moment,' says Lynn, 'Okay?'

'Yes,' says Philip. He sniffs, sets his breakfast on the floor and grasps *the Observer*. He's frowning. Dear dear. One can tell he's disappointed that the toast wasn't there, ready. On the tray at the same time as his egg.

'Here we are,' says Lynn coming back, 'Sorry for the delay; our toaster's broken.'

'Thanks,' says Philip, but he's reached an interesting article so he doesn't look up. Lynn tips the toast onto his sideplate.

'More coffee Robert?' she says.

'No thank you.' Actually I could murder a cup. I say this because I'm embarrassed.

'Okay,' says Lynn as she leaves.

I stare at my book. There is laughter from the radio in the kitchen. A panel game. I picture the studio audience in tidy rows, adoring the celebs, laughing on demand. Then riding home to Chigwell on the tube and telling the neighbours how funny it was. I watch Philip. He reads. And reads. He's not touching his breakfast yeah. After about a minute I put on my sarcastic voice. I say:

'I don't think Lynn is coming to butter your toast for you.'

He glares across at me. One can tell he's upset because he gets this twitch above his right eyebrow.

Still in my sarcastic voice I say: 'You might just have to butter it yourself dear.' Then I stick my head back in my book sharpish because he looks like he might burst into tears. That's all we need. Good Lord.

After a moment, I hear him grunt, hoisting the tray onto his lap; then there's a tapping noise as he probes the egg. When I look up, Philip isn't crying, he's inserting a hectare of toast into his mouth. His lips protrude, like he's wearing an African tribal accessory. He breathes loudly through his nose; one hand cups his chin in case anything drops onto his front. Only him and this breakfast exist.

When the food is all gone, he jiggles crumbs from his shirt onto the tray and returns it to the floor. He attacks the cross-word.

Dave pops his head round. 'Cheerio now,' he says. Poor lamb works on Sunday. 'Lynn's getting dressed. See you both again soon.'

'I'll look forward to that,' says Philip, with a queenly wave from his chair. There's a great smear of egg yolk across his chin.

'Bye,' I say. As the front door clicks, I feel an acorn of pain in my gut.

Philip frowns into the paper. Soon, he'll spend some considerable time on the loo. The larger the man the longer the toilet-time yeah, so I've found. I go out and start the dishes. Might as well. While the basin fills with water, I worry about this pain. I'm just hoping it's not an ulcer.

Janet Paisley   *1991*

DUE

It's early moarnin an the mist's risin aff the gress, hingin ablow
the trees like a curtin fae thur branches. It suits me. Ah'm no
in masell. A coo lous wi burth pain faur doon the holla. A wey
aff fae cauvin, bit kennin it. Ma feet ur sodden yit thurs nae
mindin in me. Mibbe the harr is passin through me tae.

    Only the shoatgun is soalid. Heaviur, greyur, cauldur.
Soalid, richt enough. It cairryin me. Cairryin me doon the field,
ower the burn's ruckled stanes, through its white watter an up
by the mill.

    Thurs nae a sowl aboot an ah leuk back tae see a licht cum
oan in yin hoose. Rab Coannell gittin up fur the post. Ah keep
ahint the mill, doon tae the coattages. The weeds ur high here
an thur wetness wid tie thum room me. Ye jist keep shuvin.

    Ootside his hoose thurs nae back gairden. Jist the wildness
an the wet. Close tae the stanes huv the braith o the wurld oan
thum. A licht goes oan it ma shouder, dull yella. Watter rins,
tinny, intae a kettle. Thur is whustlin. Saft, nae tune, mind else-
whaur whustlin. Ah dinnae waant these meenuts o his day. The
waashin. The tea made, drunk. Ah waant the slammin o his
door. Feet oan his graivel path. The key in his gairidge pad-loak.
Ah waant the leuk oan his face is he turns roon.

Marianne Carey   *1992*

ONE WAY

Driving along the motorway,
Heading for the second exit after the
Grey corrugated shed with Mr Happy on the side,
A man in a red hatch-back
Drove right up the inside and
He looked so bad-tempered
I lost the place and drove
Straight over the chevrons.
Well that was it.
I couldn't face another motorway slip road
So I just stayed where I was,
In the middle lane doing sixty
Till my petrol ran out,
Two miles north of
Ecclefechan.

A.L. Kennedy *1992*

A MEDITATION UPON PENGUINS

Of those who look upon the world of wonders, of those who would see miracles and light, how many have bid their gaze seek out the penguin? And yet did they all; philosophers, warriors, saints; but occupy themselves a little moment in the study of this paragon of birds would not their labours flourish, enriched a thousand times and then a thousand?

Reader, I beg your patience, I beg this fragment from the time which makes your life that I might reveal some shadow of penguin's glory and the good wisdom of its Path. Trust in me as you would trust a penguin – for who in the deep honesty of his heart may ever say he was betrayed by any penguin – and surely, even this selfless giving of your time and trust bears us an example and first step upon the Path. **Without time for their observation and trust to bring them forth there can come no miracles.** Not with the aid of all the penguins on earth.

It may be a man will cry out, 'But what am I to the penguin and what is the penguin to me?' My answer is as simple as rain: it falls straight. Perhaps you may feel you are distant from the penguin, does this mean you can take no delight in it? When your love is separated from you and in another place, will you love her no more? When you know the stars are untold miles away and not painted on a close roof of a sky, will they cease to glimmer and give joy? **It is not the duty of any living thing to have place in its heart for any other living thing, be it the worm turning in the earth, or the prisoner in his chains?**

Is there not a further lesson borne by the joyful, Southern bird for our race, the Scots? May we, a people at once above and below all other peoples, not learn that there is a place for us in the great sea of humanity, that we may dive and mingle in it and still not be lost. Remember, like the penguin, may not a Scot be welcome anywhere?

Here, we may also learn that **good things may be sought out with the generous assistance of reflection.** If a man seeks to be near a penguin, he may transport himself across the globe to sit with one on the great ice. Or he may go to the zoo and find one there. He may judge for himself which is the more simple task.

As to the presence of an indissoluble relation between humanity and the penguin, I leave my reader's sure judgement and measured reflection to sift out the truth. As we know, **sure and sifted measurement, measured and sifted sureness and surely measuring siftness all bring on truth.**

Now perhaps a woman may ask, 'How can there be untold wonders concealed in what is, after all, a short and comical, fishy bird?' My answer is short as the penguin itself. **Wonders there are.**

For is not the penguin a bird and yet does it not fly in water not in air, teaching us that **all is possible?** Even for a Scot.

We may see how will and water have smoothed and narrowed the natural feathers of a bird into the almost fur of a penguin, clothing it perfectly against the snow and tempests of its chosen home. The feet of the penguin, though forever naked against such terrible things as icebergs and the bitterness of cold, salt sea, never trouble it for a moment, so fitted are they for their purpose. How equally fit are its wings for swimming, its beak for fishing, its bright eye for discerning white across white. Thus the penguin teaches us of the full rightness and kindness of our world. Deny your relatives, your teachers, the queer twist in your stomach when you wake with the dawn, inexcusably alive – **even to us, the world may be kind.**

And the penguin will also show us, a wandering race, that to stray in arrogance beyond our native place may bring us griefs we never dreamed of. Imagine, reader, the penguin's torment if it was, all at once, arboreally inclined; its pitiful scrambles at mighty trunks, its patterings off leafy branches. What would become of the penguin lost in forests, or indeed, in the rasp and wither of Ghobi sands? Before we ourselves begin such momentous movements and translations we must be sure to equip ourselves for that which may reasonably befall. Preparedness is all. **A penguin with a rope and crampons may climb a tree.**

And is there not a special message for all in the very snows that hem about the penguin? Are we not very specially conjoined with the noble creature in choosing, like it, to live somewhere both movingly picturesque and tragically rich in rheumatic and sinus complaints? Let our nation take pride not in wealth or dominion, but in this.

We may also remember the penguin has no money, neither clothing, nor true shelter and yet it stands proud. **Who has ever seen the penguin stoop?** But, Sir, remember also that men and women, though bound in their souls with a sympathy for the penguin, are not themselves in any way penguins, though many have mistaken them for such. Despite the actions and assertions of many otherwise excellent minds, we must say, 'A woman or a man may not survive, even in soft grass and gentle sun, without the benefit of shelter, food and money. Without even the natural dignity we may observe in the deportment of our treasured beast, a simple human being may fade and die.' Good reader, let not this common error cloud your thought. **A person is not a penguin and cannot be made so.**

Yet may we not aspire to the penguin's joy? Have we not seen it slip with its fellows down its icy slides to bob in the sea, then gaily scramble up to slip again? It will clatter beaks and run in the wind with a light heart. **A heart as light as the penguin's is a thing to be wished for.** And be mindful that this light heart is sustained not by the staple diet of the Scot – the potato, the oat and the fish – but by the staple diet of the penguin – fish alone. **A light heart on only fish.** This, too, is possible, but we may be proud that, despite the lightness and satisfaction of its wintery life and plain fare, the penguin may be seen across the globe from Spain to California in zoological gardens where it may taste the luxury of sun, hail observing humanity and yet still take pleasure in the simplicity of fish. This is the balance constantly maintained within the penguin. **Luxury and simplicity – we may have both.**

But the penguin does not give us pride in balance without humility and right gratitude. Even the littlest child cannot be insensible to a fitting humility when it breaks the simplest egg at breakfast time and then considers that this very egg might have brought forth a whole, new penguin; bold and free. Perhaps the egg had, in reality, only hidden the start of a chicken or duck – **we know the potential is all.** Equally, we may have gratitude that we have not been born a chicken or duck, nor yet boiled to make a breakfast. It is a sad and shameful fact that men have fed upon penguins in dark hours. We should be grateful that penguins have never been moved to feed upon men. We should be humbled by our former wickedness and determined that we shall be vigilant to prevent the return of any trace of like abominations. As the Penguin Path will often remind us, **mind what you eat.**

Consider an instant, reader, the land of the penguin; the white, flat white of the penguin's home. Consider now the coloration of the penguin itself. 'How can it be that the penguin is both white and black?' a seeker on the path may inwardly ask. 'What may this signify?'

Here is a nice confusion. Surely like the polar bear, like milk, the penguin should be wholly white that it might be rendered safely invisible in its cold surrounds. But no. Things are quite otherwise and they are so with a purpose. There is a lesson here on the Path; perhaps the hardest lesson of them all.

Notice that if the penguin should lie upon its face, turning its back upon the whole arc of the world, only the blackness of its feathers may be seen, marking out the glorious bird, exposing it entirely to foes of every kind. And yet, should the penguin lie upon its back, bearing its vital organs and the red tenderness of its heart to all that come, then is the whiteness of its belly feathers lost in the whiteness of the snow. Thus does the penguin, in embracing Nature, find itself protected by that very Nature and gentle Power which surrounds it. **Embrace life freely, Scot, and see how freely it returns your favour.** Being ever mindful that a penguin does not often lie down, in either direction.

Oh, reader, think of the Southern winds in the penguin's feathers: that sound we may never hear, but may imagine. Know that there is nothing we may not learn, in putting ourselves within the triangular web prints of the noble and courageous penguin. What goodness and example may we not find there? Name me the penguin which has burned down a listed building by carelessly smoking in bed? Point me out the mocker of elderly ladies, the jumper of queues, the giver of previously sucked boiled sweets to little children who ever was revealed to be a penguin. What war has a penguin started? What excellent new plan for economic reformation has ever been imposed by any penguin?

Think. Who would die for a penguin, kill for a penguin, offer a penguin their vote? No one. And is that not the finest and last lesson on the Path? It is indeed. Join with me, reader, in the fervent hope that our rich and our powerful, our leaders and our led, our elected and our despots might imitate the virtues of the penguin. Let none die or kill or vote for any one of them. Lift up your cries that the penguin; the obscure, the fishy, the mocked; the shorter than average penguin might become the phoenix of all lands. And let us begin the Path here. Let fly the Penguin Rampant! Let fly all!

Brian McCabe   *1992*

NOT ABOUT THE KIDS

He could just remember the apples and oranges careering
around the kitchen. And the grapes – that's right, he'd just
bought those grapes in the afternoon. He'd picked up a bunch
of them in the fruit shop and felt their luxurious weight in his
hand, half wondering if they could really afford them, what
with being unemployed, and half thinking that the kids hardly
ever got grapes. The way they'd scattered all over the floor –
ricocheting around the kitchen like the beads of a broken neck-
lace! In his anger he'd scooped the fruitbowl off the table and,
in one sweeping movement, flung it at the wall. It exploded.
Thank Christ the kids hadn't been there. He had to make sense
of what had happened, or else here he was, driving through the
night with no real clue about why he was here, in the middle of
nowhere in Fife.

A light rain was beginning to fall and he switched on the
wipers. He stared at the road in front of him. He was driving. He
had to keep his mind on the road. It felt like he'd been driving
for a long time, for years and years of his life. Now the road
seemed to be coming at him out of the night, negotiating him
rather than the other way round, as if it was testing him. If he
could just concentrate on driving this car along this road, maybe
all the other stuff would sort itself out. He'd had a row with his
wife and now he was driving. That was all there was to it.

He braked to take a corner and heard the grinding screech
of metal on metal. The brake-pads needed to be changed
months ago. Now the discs would be scuppered. The shocks
needed to be replaced as well, and one of the rear coil-springs
was broken. Age, the guy at the garage had told him, looking at
him, not the car. But he hadn't had the money to go ahead and
get the work done there and then. At any moment the broken
spring could leap out, and the car collapse on to the rear axle.

It had been something so trivial, of course, some trivial little
thing they'd disagreed about, not about the kids but about the
housework – the household chores! Ruth had started getting at
him about putting the rubbish out – was that how it had *started*?
He'd been sitting there at the table, after the communal family
meal. Bobby had been obstreperous as usual, throwing his food
on the floor, insisting on drinking out of a glass like everyone

else, then spilling his juice all over the table. Emma had been finicky and difficult and the food – an experimental fish curry – hadn't gone down well. She'd interrupted them with endless questions every time they'd tried to speak to each other. There had been a bottle of wine – his idea, along with the grapes. Ruth had declined the wine wearily, saying it was a waste of money. Maybe it had started with the wine, with the waste of money.

And, when the table had been cleared, with Bobby on his knee, popping a grape or two into the boy's mouth, he'd been aware of Ruth making more of a thing of doing the dishes than usual. The plates were crashing and colliding in the sink and she was smashing handfuls of cutlery down on the metal draining board. He'd asked her what the fuck was wrong with her. Nothing was wrong with her, she'd said, but in a tone of voice that seethed with resentment. Then she'd started sweeping the kitchen floor and shouting at Emma to get out from under her feet.

When he thought about it now, it came clearer that what he'd been trying to do was to woo her, but he'd tried to include the kids, when what was needed was not about the kids. What was needed was something else. And it was as if she held him responsible for trying but failing, as if the attempt had reminded her of how things could be but were not. The way she'd swept that floor, like some vengeful Cinderella.

Leave it, he'd said, just fucking leave it and I'll do it later on. Then she'd started dealing with the rubbish, tugging that black bag out of the bucket, tying it up so tightly. What was she trying to tell him? That he was neglecting this twice-weekly fucking ritual, normally earmarked as a chore of his in the demarcation of labour between them? She'd deliberately done one of his chores, encroached on his territory, so that she could get at him about it – could this be true?

He'd picked up Bobby and grabbed Emma by the arm and made for the door. Ruth had shouted something at him about the way he was handling the kids. Christ Almighty. He'd shouted back at her: No, this is not about the kids, this has nothing to do with the kids! So he'd removed them from the battlefield, running their bath and putting them in it before returning to wage war with Ruth about the rubbish. He'd tried to take over but she'd resisted and the two of them had ended up having a tug of war with the rubbish bag. It had split and all the food scraps and nappies and tin cans and eggshells had spilled on the floor, the floor she'd just swept. They'd stopped everything then to argue savagely. Then he'd smashed the fruitbowl and stamped out of the house, slamming the door. It was awful, it was desperate. But what was it all about?

He was finding it hard to concentrate on driving. He kept thinking of all the things he should've said but hadn't found the words for, the reasonable, rational things... He came to a bend so sharp that he had to slow down to a crawl to take it. He didn't know this road and it kept surprising him, dipping and rising and twisting into the night unpredictably. He couldn't go back tonight, that was for certain. Maybe this time he wouldn't go back at all, maybe this was it, the final break, and they'd both remember this night like no other night in their lives.

Up ahead, just beyond the range of his dipped headlights, there was some kind of truck. One of its brake lights wasn't working. A truck or a lorry? It was hard to make out on that dark road. Even when he flicked his headlights on full for a moment, it was difficult to determine the exact nature of the vehicle. A loose tarpaulin was roped around the cargo, whatever it was. At every sudden summit, the truck made a lot of noise, as if its various parts had come apart for a second, only to crash back together as the truck roared on into the night. The way it seemed to veer from side to side unpredictably at every bend bothered him. He put his foot on the accelerator. He felt his heartbeat speeding up too. He knew that if Ruth had been in the car with him he wouldn't take the risk – but she wasn't.

Before he could level with the truck he saw, above the dark embankment at the side of the road, the light from an approaching car's headlights, so he braked and pulled back in. The bastard hadn't slowed down to let him pass – hadn't he stepped on it to make sure he couldn't? The approaching car dipped its headlights as it came round the corner. Even so, it dazzled him and he slowed down till it had passed. There was a moment when he could make out nothing but the red brake-light of the truck, dancing around in the night ahead, a taunting spark, then it disappeared. When his eyes had readjusted he saw that he was too far into the middle of the road as he took the bend, so he swung back out. This road was wild. It wasn't so much the blind summits or the hairpin bends, but the stretches in between, where the road wavered and couldn't make up its mind which way to go.

It was a dangerous road. Maybe it didn't go anywhere. He lit a cigarette and tugged open the overflowing ashtray on the dashboard. He'd been smoking too much and there was a sour taste in his mouth that reminded him of nights years ago, when he and Ruth had started up together, when they'd stayed up most of the night and gone to bed at dawn, making love as the birds were singing outside...

He came over a rise and saw the truck there ahead, its one brake light jiggling up and down, its tail-board rattling. It had slowed down. There was a clear stretch ahead. He accelerated and signalled to overtake, but it was taking longer than it should. The truck threw a spray of dirty rainwater over his windscreen and snarled at him as he drew level with it. He could feel the car jogging around on the uneven road. It was a relief to get in front. Even so, the truck-driver had his headlights at full beam and he could see nothing but the glare of them in his mirror. The truck was gaining on him, so he put the foot down again and tried to leave it behind.

A sharp bend in the road came at him and he had to brake hard to get round it. The brakes screeched. The car skidded and swung too far into the side of the road and scraped noisily against the barrier beneath the sign with the chevrons. At the same moment he was dazzled by the headlights of an oncoming car and he raised his right hand to shield his eyes, trying to right the wheel with his left hand. The other car roared past blaring its horn.

He went on driving, but his heart was hammering and he could feel his hands and his arms shaking. He had to stop somewhere as soon as possible.

As if the road had taken this decision, it wound downwards and showed him a speed-limit sign and the nameplate of a village he'd never heard of. He slowed down until he saw a pub just off the main street, then pulled over and waited till the truck roared past. It was just a truck, moving something from somewhere to somewhere else in the night. He put his hand to his head, pressing his thumb and his forefinger into his eyelids, and he sat like this for a moment before switching off the engine and the lights.

There were only a few people in the pub and he felt conspicuous as he walked to the bar. He was a stranger, and they didn't often get strangers here. They stared at him with hostile curiosity. Some of them seemed to dismiss him quickly, as if they knew he was from the city and had just had a row with his wife.

The barman took too long to serve him. He was serving somebody else but taking his time about it, having a conversation with some of the men sitting round the bar. Apparently they were talking about birds, birds they found living in the eaves of their houses. One man was maintaining that when swifts made their nests they used their spit to hold them together, and that swift's spit was the main ingredient in bird's-nest soup.

He ordered a double and asked if there was a telephone. The barman pointed to the door that led to the toilets. He took his drink to a table by the window and drank half of it and smoked a cigarette. He thought about what he should say to her.

Ruth, it was the way you swept the floor.

Ruth, I demand custody of the kids.

Ruth, I think you should have custody of the kids. They can come to me half the week and stay with you the other half.

Ruth, we need to talk. Not about the kids. About us. What's happening to *us*, Ruth?

He looked at the only woman in the bar, as if this might help him to think of what he should say to his wife. She was sitting on a high stool up at the bar, next to a man – her husband? She wore a tailored leather jacket, the collar of which she held between her finger and thumb to illustrate her point. The man shook his head, raised his eyebrows wearily and slouched on his stool, over which he'd slung his nylon jerkin. They seemed a sad couple, trapped in their coupledom. But maybe they weren't a couple at all. And if they were a couple – what did that mean, exactly, when you got down to it?

The others sitting at the bar all seemed to know each other, though some wore muddied work boots and dungarees, others sports jackets or suits. Over in the far corner, two younger men in jeans and tee-shirts were playing pool and listening to the juke-box.

He took his drink and his cigarettes out to the telephone with him.

It rang and rang. Had she unplugged the phone? Eventually she answered:

– It's me.

– Oh.

– Sorry about the fruitbowl.

– So am I – not just about the fruitbowl.

– I know it isn't just about the fruitbowl. I'll get you another one exactly the same.

– Like hell you will. It was an antique.

– I know, I know, it's irreplaceable. I'm sorry. The thing is, I was angry.

– You were angry. Right. That explains everything, doesn't it? You were angry so you threw the fruitbowl at the wall. If the kids had been there –

– They weren't. I made sure of that.

– They could have been. Anyway *I* was there.

He apologised again then waited until she spoke.

– Where are you?

– Fife.

– What the hell are you doing in Fife?

– I don't know, I drove here.

– You must be out of your mind.

– I am. I am totally out of my mind.

– You're drunk.

– No, not yet.

– You're driving.

– That's right. I'm driving.

– You must be crazy.

– At this moment, you're right, I am completely crazy.

She didn't reply to that. He waited a minute, then said:

– What's it about?

– What?

– All this. What's it all about?

– What do you think it's all about?

– That's what I'm asking you.

She sighed with fatigue and said wearily that she didn't know. He was glad she didn't. That gave him the initiative:

– It's something to do with me losing my job, isn't it?

– No. Of course not.

– I'm around the house too much. We're with each other all the time. I mean, sometimes a person has to go away just so that they can come back.

– Don't come back. Not tonight.

– Don't worry, I won't.

– I don't want to talk anymore. I'm tired, I want to go to bed.

– I'll tell you a bed-time story, then. Once upon a time, there was a boy and a girl, and they fell madly in love with each other. But they were young, just kids –

– I've heard this story before.

– Not this one, Ruth, this one is not about us, this one is

about these kids, these kids who fell madly in love. In those days, Ruth, it was as simple as that. We're talking about a time when people went out with each other for a month, if it was serious. But these kids are so in love they manage to go on for a year, more than a year... That gives you some idea how serious about each other they are. But, as I was saying, they're young, too young to really know how to *go on* being in love, if you know what I mean, and after a while something has to happen.

The pips sounded, and he hurriedly pulled a handful of coins from his pocket, dumped them on the shelf and searched among them for a ten pence. He found one and put it in just as they were about to be cut off.

– Ruth? Are you still there?

– What's the point of all this?

– So, and this is the sad bit of the story, there comes a point when the boy begins to feel restless, he feels the need for change... He's changing anyway, he's growing up, and the whole world is changing round about him. And so one night, out of the blue, the boy tells the girl he wants to finish with her. So they split up. Some time passes. The boy is totally miserable without the girl, but he is alone. He's himself and only himself. Then he goes back to her, and she takes him back with open arms. And they go on together again, pretty much as before except that everything has changed. In fact, nothing is ever quite the same after that brief separation. And soon the girl begins to feel restless, she feels the need for change...

– You got what you deserved. What d'you want, sympathy?

All I'm saying is sometimes people need the threat of separation, I mean so they can go on. The threat has to be real. But as soon as it is real it will never go away, it will always be there. D'you know what I'm saying, Ruth?

– You're saying it's time to split up.

– I never said that.

– Maybe we should.

– Just remember it was you who suggested it first.

– What does it matter who suggests it first?

– It matters. Everything matters.

– Don't sound so gloomy about it.

– How should I sound – cheerful?

– I'm not saying that.

– What are you saying?

– I'm not saying anything.

– Well, why not? Are we communicating with each other here or what?

– I'm tired of communicating. We can communicate tomorrow.

– What about tomorrow?

But he could feel her attention slipping away from him. He tried to hold it.

– Are the kids okay?

– They're asleep, if that's what you mean.

– That isn't what I mean.

– What do you mean then?

– I mean are they okay? Come on, you know what I mean.

– They're okay, yes.

– Christ Ruth, I was trying tonight. I tried with the meal, I tried with the kids, I tried with us...

– I know you tried. D'you think I haven't been trying? I'm always trying. Maybe that's the problem. Maybe it's just too much effort.

– You sound exhausted, Ruth.

– I am. My period's come.

– D'you think that had something to do with it?

– How do I know? Maybe, maybe not.

The pips went. He tried to tell her that he'd call her again in the morning, but he was cut off.

He took his drink back to the bar, finished it and ordered another. No one seemed to pay him any attention now, and they had become a meaningless blur to him. He didn't want to look at them, so he sat down in a chair that faced the window. He stared at his distorted image reflected in the marbled glass, and when he moved his head a little, his features disintegrated horribly.

Her period? Maybe, maybe not. But what, really, had happened? Maybe nothing had really happened. Maybe the threat was all that was needed. But then, maybe what he'd said to her was true: once the threat was there, it would never really go away.

If she could be here with him now... but all that lay ahead was the night, a night spent alone, in a bed-and-breakfast in Fife. The utter pointlessness of it made him bang his glass down on the table as he finished his drink. Someone laughed at the bar, and he thought he heard a low-toned comment from one of the tables. He closed his eyes and listened. The clack of the pool

balls, the music from the juke-box, the voices – all the noises in
the bar seemed to swell inside him and engulf him, until he felt
adrift in the world. He had to get out.

It had stopped raining, and the night was cool and clear.
He walked to the car but didn't get in. He leaned against it and
looked along the dark street of the village, at the haphazard
silhouette of the rooftops. He imagined the swifts in the eaves,
their nests being held together by spit, their eggs... It reminded
him vaguely of his childhood, although he had never lived in
such a place.

Dilys Rose   *1992*

ALL THE LITTLE LOVED ONES

I love my kids. My husband too, though sometimes he asks me
whether I do, asks the question, Do you still love me? He asks
it while I am in the middle of rinsing spinach or loading washing into the machine, or chasing a trail of toys across the
kitchen floor. When he asks the question at a time like that, it's
like he's speaking an ancient, forgotten language. I can remember a few isolated words but can't connect them, can't get the
gist, don't know how to answer. Of course I could say, Yes I
love you, still love you, of course I still love you. If I didn't still
love you I wouldn't be here, would I, wouldn't have hung
around just to go through the motions of companionship and
sex. Being alone never bothered me. It was something I chose.
Before I chose you. But of course, that is not accurate. Once
you become a parent there is no longer a simple equation.

We have three children. All our own. Blood of our blood,
flesh of our flesh etc., delivered into our hands in the usual way,
a slithering mess of blood and slime and wonder, another tiny
miracle.

In reply to his question my husband really doesn't want to
hear any of my irritating justifications for sticking around, my
caustic logic. He doesn't really want to hear anything at all.
The response he wants is a visual and tactile one. He wants me
to drop the spinach, the laundry, the toys, sweep my hair out of
my eyes, turn round, away from what I'm doing and look at
him, look lovingly into his dark, demanding eyes, walk across
the kitchen floor – which needs to be swept again – stand over
him as he sits at the table fingering a daffodil, still bright in its
fluted centre but crisp and brown at the edges, as if it's been
singed. My husband wants me to cuddle up close.

Sometimes I can do it, the right thing, what's needed. Other
times, when I hear those words it's like I've been turned to mar-
ble or ice, to something cold and hard and unyielding. I can't
even turn my head away from the sink, far less walk those few
steps across the floor. I can't even think about it. And when he
asks, What are you thinking? Again I'm stuck. Does it count as
thinking to be considering whether there is time to bring down
the laundry from the pulley to make room for the next load
before I shake off the rinsing water, pat the leaves dry, chop off

the stalks and spin the green stuff around the magimix? That's usually what my mind is doing, that is its activity and if it can be called thinking, then that's what I'm doing. Thinking about something not worth relating.

What are you thinking?

Nothing. I'm not thinking about anything.

Which isn't the same thing. Thinking about nothing means mental activity, a focusing of the mind on the fact or idea of nothing and that's not what I am doing. I've no interest in that kind of activity, no time for it, no time to ponder the true meaning of life, the essential nature of the universe and so on. Such speculation is beyond me. Usually when I'm asked what I'm thinking my mind is simply vacant and so my reply is made with a clear, vacant conscience.

I'm approaching a precipice. Each day I'm drawn nearer to the edge. I look only at the view. I avoid looking at the drop but I know what's there. At least, I can imagine it. I don't want to be asked either question, the conversation must be kept moving, hopping across the surface of our lives like a smooth flat stone.

... Thought is not the point. I am feeling it, the flush, the rush of blood, the sensation of, yes, swooning. It comes in waves. Does it show? I'm sure it must show on my face the way pain might, the way pain would show on my husband's face...

Do you still love me? What are you thinking?

Tonight I couldn't even manage my usual, Nothing. It wouldn't come out right, I try it out in my head, practise it, imagine the word as it would come out. It would sound unnatural, false, a strangled, evasive mumble or else a spat denial. Either way it wouldn't pass. It would lead to probing. A strained, suspicious little duet would begin in the midst of preparing the dinner and I know where this edgy, halting tune leads, I know the notes by heart.

(Practice makes perfect. Up and down the same old scales until you can do them without tripping up, without twisting fingers or breaking resolutions, without swearing, yelling, failing or resentment at the necessity of repetition. Without scales the fingers are insufficiently developed to be capable of... until you can do it in your sleep, until you *do* do it in your sleep, up and down as fast as dexterity permits. Without practice, life skills also atrophy.)

For years we've shared everything we had to share, which

wasn't much at first and now is way too much. In the way of possessions at least. We started simply: one room, a bed we nailed together from pine planks and lasted a decade; a few lingering relics from previous couplings (and still I long to ditch that nasty little bronze figurine made by the woman before me. A troll face, with gouged-out eyes. Scary at night, glowering from a corner of the bedroom). Money was scarce but new love has no need of money. Somewhere to go, to be together is all and we were lucky. We had that. Hell is love with no place to go.

While around us couples were splitting at the seams, we remained intact. In the midst of break-ups and breakouts, we tootled on, sympathetic listeners, providers of impromptu pasta, a pull-out bed for the night, the occasional alibi. We listened to the personal disasters of our friends but wondered, in private, in bed, alone together at the end of another too-late night, what all the fuss was about. Beyond our ken, all that heartbreak, all that angst. What did it have to do with us, our lives, our kids? We had no room for it. Nor, for that matter, a great deal of space for passion.

An example to us all, we've been told, You two are an example to us all. Of course it was meant to be taken with a pinch of salt, a knowing smile but said frequently enough for the phrase to stick, as if our friends in their cracked, snapped, torn-to-shreds state, our friends who had just said goodbye to someone they loved, or someone they didn't love after all or any more, as if all of them were suddenly united in a wilderness of unrequited love. While we, in our dusty, cluttered home, had achieved something other than an accumulation of consecutive time together.

This is true, of course, and we can be relied upon to provide some display of the example that we are. My husband is likely to take advantage of the opportunity and engage in a bit of public necking. Me, I sling mud, with affection. Either way, between us we manage to steer the chat away from our domestic compatibility, top up our friends' drinks, turn up the volume on the stereo, stir up a bit of jollity until it's time to say Goodnight. See you soon. Look after yourself, until it's time to be left alone together again with our example. Our differences remain.

Do you still love me? What are you thinking?

Saturday night. The children are asleep. Three little dark

heads are thrown back on pillows printed with characters from Lewis Carroll, Disney and Masters of the Universe. Three little mouths blow snores into the intimate, bedroom air. Upstairs, the neighbours hammer tacks into a carpet, their dogs romp and bark, their antique plumbing gurgles down the wall but the children sleep on, their sweet breath rising and falling in unison.

We are able to eat in peace, take time to taste the food which my husband has gone to impressive lengths to prepare. The dinner turns out to be an unqualified success: the curry is smooth, spicy, aromatic, the rice dry, each grain distinct, each firm little ellipse brushing against the tongue. The dinner is a joy and a relief. My husband is touchy about his cooking and requires almost as much in the way of reassurance and compliments in this as he does about whether I still love him or not. A bad meal dampens the spirits, is distressing both to the cook and the cooked-for. A bad meal can be passed over, unmentioned but not ignored. The stomach too has longings for more than simply to be filled. A bad meal can be worse than no meal at all.

But it was an extremely good meal and I was wholehearted and voluble in my appreciation. Everything was going well. We drank more wine, turned off the overhead light, lit a candle, fetched the cassette recorder from the kids' room and put on some old favourites; smoochy, lyrical, emotive stuff, tunes we knew so well we didn't have to listen, just let them fill the gaps in our conversation. So far so good.

Saturdays have to be good. It's pretty much all we have. Of us, the two of us just. One night a week, tiptoeing through the hall so as not to disturb the kids, lingering in the kitchen because it's further away from their bedroom than the living room, we can speak more freely, don't need to keep the talk turned down to a whisper. We drink wine and catch up. It is necessary to catch up, to keep track of each other.

Across the country, while all the little loved ones are asleep, wives and husbands, single parents and surrogates are sitting down together or alone, working out what has to be done. There are always things to be done, to make tomorrow pass smoothly, to make tomorrow work. I look through the glasses and bottles and the shivering candle flame at my husband. The sleeves of his favourite shirt – washed-out blue with pearly buttons, last year's Christmas present from me – are rolled up. His elbows rest on the table which he recently sanded and polished by hand. It took forever. We camped out in the living room while coat after coat of asphyxiating varnish was applied. It looks good now, better than before. But was the effort worth the effect?

My husband's fine pale fingers are pushed deep into his hair. I look past him out of the kitchen window, up the dark sloping street at parked cars and sodium lights, lit windows and smoking chimneys, the blinking red eye of a plane crossing a small trough of blue-black sky. My house is where my life happens. In it there is love, work, a roof, a floor, solidity, houseplants, toys, pots and pans, achievements and failures, inspirations and mistakes, recipes and instruction booklets, guarantees and spare parts, plans, dreams, memories. And there is no need, nothing here pushing me. It is nobody's fault.

I go to playparks a lot, for air, for less mess in the house and of course because the kids like to get out. Pushing a swing, watching a little one arcing away and rushing back to your hands, it's natural to talk to another parent. It passes the time. You don't get so bored pushing, the little one is kept lulled and amenable. There's no way of reckoning up fault or blame or responsibility, nothing is stable enough, specific enough to be held to account and that's not the point. The swing swung back, I tossed my hair out of my eyes and glanced up at a complete stranger, a father. The father smiled back.

We know each other's names, the names of children and spouses. That's about all. We ask few questions. No need for questions. We meet and push our children on swings and sometimes we stand just close enough for our shoulders to touch, just close enough to feel that fluttering hollowness, like hunger. We visit the park – even in the rain, to watch the wind shaking the trees and tossing cherry blossoms on to the grass, the joggers and dog walkers lapping the flat green park – to be near each other.

Millions have stood on this very same ledge, in the privacy of their own homes, the unweeded gardens of their minds. Millions have stood on the edge and tested their balance, their common sense, strength of will, they have reckoned up the cost, in mess and misery, have wondered whether below the netless drop a large tree with spread branches awaits to cushion their fall. So simple, so easy. All I have to do is rock on my heels, rock just a shade too far and we will all fall down. Two husbands, two wives and all the little loved ones.

Iain Crichton Smith   *1992*

THE BRIDGE

My wife and I met them in Israel. They were considerably
younger than us and newly married. They came from Devon
and they had a farm which they often talked about. For some
reason they took a fancy to us, and were with us a fair amount
of the time, sometimes on coach trips, sometimes at dinner in
the evening. They were called Mark and Elaine.

I didn't like Israel as much as I had expected I would. I read
the *Jerusalem Post* regularly, and was disturbed by some of the
stories I found there, though the paper itself was liberal enough.
There were accounts of the beatings of Palestinians, and pictures
of Israeli soldiers who looked like Nazis.

Certainly it was interesting to see Bethlehem, Nazareth, the
Garden of Gethsemane, and they reminded me of the security
of my childhood: but at the same time seemed physically tatty,
and without romance. Also we were often followed, especially
in Jerusalem, by Arab school-children who tried to sell us post-
cards: the schools were in fact shut by official order.

Though this was the first time Mark and Elaine were abroad
they were brighter than us with regard to money. Mark had a
gift for finding out the best time for exchanging sterling and
was, I thought, rather mean. Sometimes we had coffee in a four-
some during the day or at night, and he would pull his purse out
very carefully and count out the money: he never gave a tip. He
was also very careful about buying for us exactly what we had
bought for him on a previous occasion. On the other hand he
bought his wife fairly expensive rings which she flourished
expansively. They walked hand in hand. They were both tall
and looked very handsome.

One day the coach took us to the Golan Heights. There were
red flowers growing there, and some abandoned tanks were
lying in a glade. The guide, who was a Jew originally from Iraq,
told us that a few tanks had held off the attacks till the reservists
had been called up. 'They can be called up very quickly,' he said.
It was very peaceful, looking across the valley to the other side
but there were notices about unexploded mines.

Often we met young boys and girls on the buses. They
hitched rides from place to place in their olive green uniforms.
They were of the age of schoolboys and schoolgirls. One morn-

ing on a bus I heard a girl listening to a pop song on a radio that she carried with her. It seemed very poignant and sad.

I used to talk quite a lot about articles I had read in the *Jerusalem Post*, which was my Bible because it was the only paper written in English. But neither Mark nor Elaine read much, not even the fat blockbusters that passengers on the coach sometimes carried with them. They told us a great deal about their farm, and what hard work it was. Then there was also a lot of paper work, including VAT. They were very fond of each other, and, as I have said, often walked hand in hand. He was very handsome: she was pretty enough in a healthy sort of way.

We were told by the guide a great deal about the history of Israel, about the Assyrians, about the Crusaders, about the Philistines. I especially remember a beautiful little simple Catholic church above Jerusalem. Then in Jerusalem we were shown the Via Dolorosa. At intervals along the route, young Jewish soldiers with guns were posted. 'Here is where Christ's hand rested,' said the guide, pointing to the wall. He himself had emigrated to Israel from Iraq. 'They took everything from us, even our clothes,' he said, 'for years we lived in a tent.' He had served in the paratroopers and was still liable for call-up.

We saw Masada, which was very impressive. Here the Jews had committed suicide *en masse* rather than surrender to the Romans. At one time the Israeli soldiers had been initiated into the army at a ceremony held at Masada, but that had been discontinued because of its passive associations. Thoughts of suicide were not useful against the Arabs.

I found it difficult to talk to the young couple about farming since I didn't know much about it. My wife, however, who had been brought up on a farm, chattered away about sheep, cattle, and hay. For myself I was more interested in the information I was getting from the *Jerusalem Post*. For instance, an American rabbi had said that the reason for the stone-throwing which had started was that the cinemas at Tel Aviv had been opened on a Saturday night.

We often saw Orthodox Jews wearing black hats, and beards. They sometimes read books while they were walking along the street. Also we saw many of them chanting at the Wailing Wall, where the men were separated from the women. My wife wrote a message and left it in the Wall as if it were a secret assignation. There was one comic touch: some of the

Orthodox Jews covered their hats with polythene if it was raining, as the hats were very expensive.

I read diligently in the *Jerusalem Post*. Apparently in the past there has been stone-throwing against Jews. This was in mediaeval times and when they were living in Arab countries. But though Jews complained nothing was done about it. It was considered a reasonable sport.

My wife often used to wonder why Mark and Elaine had picked us for friends since they were so much younger. Did we look cosmopolitan, seasoned travellers, or did they simply like us? Sometimes Elaine talked to my wife as if she were talking to her mother. I found it hard to talk to Mark when the women were in the shops. He often spoke about money, I noticed, and was very exact with it. I sometimes thought that it was he who looked like the seasoned traveller, since he was always totally at ease and was excellent with maps.

The two of them didn't take so many coach trips as we did. Often they went away on their own, and we only met them in the evening.

They didn't go to the Holocaust Museum with us the day we went there. The place was very quiet apart from some French schoolchildren who scampered about. My wife hissed at them to be quiet, but they only grinned insolently. There were piles of children's shoes on the floor: these had been worn by victims of the Holocaust. There were many photographs, and a film that ran all the time.

There was also a room which was in complete darkness apart from thousands of candles reflected from a range of mirrors, so that it seemed that we were under a sky of stars. A voice repeated over and over again the names of the children who had been killed. The Jews had suffered terribly, but were now in turn inflicting terror themselves.

We met a woman who had come to Israel from South Africa. She opposed the Jewish attitude to the Palestinians, though she was a Jew herself. She said that mothers everywhere were against the continued war. She herself had driven her son in her own car to the front, not during the Seven Days war but the one after it.

We were in Israel on Independence Day. Jewish planes, streaming blue and white lines of smoke behind them, formed the Jewish flag. It was very impressive and colourful but also rather aggressive.

The coach took us to a kibbutz where we were to stay for
two nights. Immediately we arrived, Mark and Elaine found
that there were cattle there, and they left us in order to find out
about the price of milk, etc.

The kibbutz itself had been raised out of a malarial swamp.
Everyone had to work, and the place looked prosperous. It
even had a beautiful theatre which the kibbutzers had built
themselves. I ordered coffee from an oldish waiter, and when I
offered him a tip he wouldn't accept it. I found out that he had
been a lieutenant-colonel on Eisenhower's staff.

The kibbutzers, we were told by the guide, had their own
problems. Sometimes when the young ones who had been reared
in a kibbutz were called up on national service they entered an
enviable world which they had not known of, and they left the
kibbutz forever. Also some Jews had accepted compensation
money from the Germans while others hadn't, and so there was
financial inequality. Thus some could afford to take holidays
while others couldn't. This introduced envy into the kibbutz.

Mark and Elaine were pleased with the cattle they had seen
and full of praise. Mark had brought a notebook with him and
had jotted down numbers of cattle, type of feeding stuff, etc.
They had been given a tour of the farm with which they had
been very happy.

One night they had told us that they recently had been in a
place in England, it might have been Dorset, and they had come
to a little bridge. There was a notice on the bridge that according to legend a couple who walked across the bridge hand in
hand would be together forever. They smiled tenderly as they
told us the story. In fact they had been on a coach trip at the
time, and the passengers on the coach had clapped as the two of
them volunteered to walk across the bridge. I thought it was a
touching little story and I could imagine the scene; on the other
hand I am not superstitious. 'How lovely,' said my wife.

My wife and I had been to Devon once. One day quite by
accident we arrived at a house which was said to be haunted,
and which had been turned into a restaurant. The owner of the
restaurant, who made full use of the legend for commercial
purposes, told us that many years before, there used to be crim-
inals who used lanterns to direct ships onto the rocks. One man
had done this only to find that one of the passengers on the
wrecked ship had been his own daughter coming home from
America. He had locked the body up in a room in his house.

Many years afterwards the farmer who now owned the house noticed a mark on the wall which suggested the existence of an extra room. He knocked the wall down and found a skeleton there. An American tourist had said that she had seen the ghost of the young girl in broad daylight, and so had been born the legend of the Haunted House. So romance and death fed money and tourism.

We told Mark and Elaine the story, which they hadn't heard before. Suddenly there was a chill in the day as I imagined the father bending down to tear the jewellery from a woman's neck and finding that it was his own daughter.

'Should you like a coffee?' I said. I saw Mark fumbling with his purse. I thought of the Samaritan Inn which had been built at the presumed point where the Good Samaritan had helped his enemy. And indeed in Israel much of the biblical story had been converted into money.

Nevertheless I couldn't love Israel. Three was too much evidence of Arab poverty. The dead bodies of Palestinian children were mixed up in my mind with the dead bodies of Jewish children. The mound of worn shoes climbed higher and higher.

On the last night of the tour we exchanged addresses. Mark and Elaine said they would write and my wife and I said we would do the same. And in fact we did do that for a while.

Today, this morning in fact, my wife received a letter from Elaine saying that she and Mark had split up. She said little, but reading between the lines we gathered that he had met a richer woman who was able to invest money in his farm.

We looked at each other for a long time, thinking of the young radiant couple who had walked hand in hand across the bridge.

Finally my wife said, 'At least they didn't have children. It would have been much worse if they had children.'

Irvine Welsh   *1992*

WHERE THE DEBRIS MEETS THE SEA

The house in Santa Monica sat tastefully back from Palisades
Beach Road, the town's bustling ocean boulevard. This was the
top end of the town, its opulence serving as the height to aspire
to for the yuppie dwellers of the condominiums further down
the Pacific coast. It was a two floored Spanish-style dwelling,
partly obscured from the road by a huge stone wall and a range
of indigenous American and imported trees. A few yards inside
the wall, an electrified security fence ran around the perimeter
of the property. Discreetly inside the gate at the entrance to the
grounds, a portable cabin was tucked, and outside it sat a burly
guard with mirror lens shades.

Wealth was certainly the overall impression given by the
property. Unlike nearby Beverly Hills, however, the concept of
wealth here seemed more utilitarian, rather than concerned
with status. The impression was that wealth was here to be
consumed, rather than flaunted ostentatiously for the purpose
of inducing respect, awe or envy.

The pool at the back of the house had been drained; this
was not a home that was occupied all the year round. Inside,
the house was expensively furnished, yet in a stark, practical
style.

Four women relaxed in a large room which led, through
patio doors, to the dry pool. They were at ease, lounging around
silently. The only sounds came from the television, which one of
them was watching, and the soft hissing of the air-conditioning
which pumped cool, dry air into the house.

A pile of glossy magazines lay on a large black coffee table.
They bore such titles as *Wideo, Scheme Scene* and *Bevvy
Merchants*. Madonna flicked idly through the magazine called
Radge, coming to an abrupt halt as her eyes feasted on the
pallid figure of Deek Prentice, resplendent in a purple, aqua
and black shell-suit.

'Phoah! Ah'd shag the erse oafay that anywey,' she lustily
exclaimed, breaking the silence, and thrusting the picture under
Kylie Minogue's nose.

Kylie inspected the image clinically, 'Hmm... ah dunno...
No bad erse oan it like, bit ah'm no really intae flat-toaps. Still,
ah widnae kick it oot ay bed, likesay, ken?'

'Whae's that?' Victoria Principal asked, filing her nails as she reclined on the couch.

'Deek Prentice fi Gilmerton. Used tae be in the casuals, bit ehs no intae that anymair,' Madonna said, popping a piece of chewing gum into her mouth.

Victoria was enthusiastic. 'Total fuckin ride. Ah bet eh's hung like a hoarse. Like that photae ah goat ay Tam McKenzie, ken fi the Young Leith Team, original seventies line-up. Fuckin welt oan it, man ah'm telling ye. Phoah, ya cunt ye! Even through the shell-suit, ye kin see ehs tackle bulgin oot. At thoat, fuck me, ah'd gie ma eye teeth tae get ma gums aroond that.'

'Ye'd probably huv tae, if ehzis big is ye say!' smirked Kylie. They all laughed loudly, except Kim Basinger, who sat curled up in a chair watching the television.

'Wishful thinkin gits ye naewhaire,' she mused. Kim was studying the sensual image of Dode Chalmers; bold shaved head, *Castlemaine Four X* t-shirt and Levis. Although Rocky, his faithful American pit-bull terrier, was not visible on the screen, Kim noted that his leather and chain leash was bound around Dode's strong, tattooed arm. The eroticism of that image was intense. She wished that she'd video-taped this programme.

The camera swung over to Rocky, whom Dode described to the interviewer as: 'My one faithful friend in life. We have an uncanny telepathy which goes beyond the archetypal man-beast relationship... in a real sense Rocky is an extension of myself.'

Kim found this a bit pretentious. Certainly, there was little doubt that Rocky was an integral part of the Dode Chalmers legend. They went everywhere together. Kim cynically wondered, however, just how much of this was a dubious gimmick, manufactured perhaps, by public relations people.

'Fuck...' gasped Kylie, open mouthed. '...what ah'd gie tae be in that dug's position now. Wearin a collar, chained tae Dode's airm. That wid dae me fine.'

'Some fuckin chance,' Kim laughed, more derisively than she'd intended.

Madonna looked across at her. 'Awright then smart cunt. Dinae you be sae fuckin smug,' she said challengingly.

'Aye Kim, dinae tell ays ye widnae git intae his keks if ye hud the chance,' Victoria sneered.

'That's whit ah sais, bit. Ah'm no gaunny git the chance, so whit good's it talkin aboot it, likesay? Ah'm in here in Southern California n Dode's ower in fuckin Leith.'

They fell into a silence, and watched Dode being inter-
viewed on *The Jimmy McGilvary Show*. Kim thought that
McGilvary was a pain in the arse, who seemed to feel that he
was as big a star as his guests. He was asking Dode about his
love-life.

'In all honesty, I don't have time for heavy relationships at
the moment. Right now I'm only interested in all the overtime
I can get. After all, one has to remember that trades fortnight
isn't that far away,' Dode explained, slightly flushed, but his
thin mouth almost curling in a smile.

'Ah'd cowp it,' Kylie licked her bottom lip.

'In a fuckin minute,' Victoria nodded severely, eyes widened.

Madonna was more interested in Deek Prentice. She turned
her attention back to the article and continued reading. She was
hoping to read something about Deek's split from the casuals.
The full story had not come out about that one, and it would
be interesting to hear Deek's side of things.

*There is hope for us all yet, as Deek is keeping an open mind
on romance since his much publicised split with sexy cinema
usherette, Sandra Riley. It's obviously an issue where Deek is
keen to set the record straight.*

*'I suppose, in a way, we loved each other too much.
There's certainly no hard feelings or bitterness on either side.
In fact, I was talking to Sandra on the phone only the other
night, so we're still the best of friends. Our respective careers
made it difficult to see as much of each other as we would have
liked. Obviously cinema isn't a nine to five thing, and furniture
removals can take me all over the country, with overnight
stays. We got used to not being together, and sort of drifted
apart. Unfortunately, it's the nature of the business we're in.
Relationships are difficult to sustain.'*

*Deek's social life is another area where he feels that he has had
more than his share of unwelcome publicity. While he makes
no secret of an enjoyment of the high life, he feels that 'certain
parties' have somewhat exaggerated things.*

*'So I enjoy the odd game of pool with Dode Chalmers and
Cha Telfer. All I can say is: guilty as charged. Yes, I'm in the
habit of visiting places like the* Spey Lounge, Swanneys *and the*
Clan Tavern; *and I enjoy a few pints of lager. However, the public only see the glamorous side. It's not as if I'm swilling away*

every night. Most evenings I'm home, watching Coronation
Street *and* East Enders. *Just to illustrate how the press get hold
of nonsense, a report appeared in a Sunday newspaper which
shall be nameless, stating that I was involved in an altercation
at a stag night in* Fox's Bar. *It's not a boozer I use, and in any
case I was working overtime that night! If I was in the pub as
often as certain gossip columnists claim, I'd hardly be able to
hold down my driving job with Northern Removals. With three
million people unemployed, I've certainly no intention of resting
on my laurels.'*

*Deek's boss, the experienced supervisor Rab Logan, agrees.
Rab probably knows Deek better than anyone in the business,
and Deek unreservedly credits the dour Leither with saving his
career. Rab told us: 'Deek came to us with a reputation for
being, should we say, somewhat difficult. He's very much an
individual, rather than a team man, and tended to go off to the
pub whenever it took his fancy. Obviously, with a flit to complete, this lack of application caused some bad feeling with the
rest of the team. We crossed swords for the first and last time,
and since then, Deek's been a joy to work with. I can't speak
highly enough of him.'*

*Deek is only too willing to acknowledge his debt to the
removal Svengali.*
    *'I owe it all to Rab. He took me aside and told me that I had
what it took to make it in the removals game. The choice was
mine. At the time I was arrogant, and nobody could tell me anything. However, I remember that exceptionally grim and lonely
journey home on the number six bus that day Rab told me a few
home truths. He has a habit of stating the transparently obvi-
ous, when you're so close to it, you can't see the woods for the
trees. After a dressing down from Rab Logan, one tends to
shape up. The lesson I learned from Rab that day was an important one. In a sense, the removal business is like any other. The
bottom line is, you're only as good as your last flit.'*
    What Deek eventually wants however, is the opportunity to

'Thirs nought tae stoap us gaun tae Leith, fir a hoaliday n
that,' Victoria suggested, tearing Madonna's attention from the
magazine.
    'Hoaliday... hoaliday...' Madonna sang.

'Aye! We could go tae the *Clan*,' Kylie enthused. 'Imagine the cock in thaire. Comin oot the fuckin waws.' She screwed up her eyes, puckered her lips and blew hard, shaking her head from side to side.

'Ye'd nivir git served in thaire,' Kim sniffed.

'Ken your problem Kim? Ye nivir think fuckin positively enough. We've goat the poppy. Dinae you sit thaire n tell ays you've no goat the hireys,' Madonna remonstrated.

'Ah nivir sais that. It's no jist aboot poppy...'

'Well then. We could go tae Leith. Huv a fuckin barry time. Hoaliday ay a lifetime,' Madonna told her then continued her singing. 'It wid be, it wid be so nice, hoaliday...'

Victoria and Kylie nodded enthusiastically in agreement. Kim looked unconvinced.

'You cunts crack ays up.' She shook her head. 'No fuckin real.'

'Whit's wrong wi your fuckin pus, ya stroppy cunt?' Madonna mouthed belligerently, sitting up in the chair. 'Ye git oan ma fuckin tits Kim, so ye do.'

'We'll nivir go tae fuckin Leith!' Kim said, in a tone of scornful dismissal. 'Youse ur fuckin dreamin.'

'Wi might go one time!' said Kylie, with just a hint of desperation in her voice. The others nodded in agreement.

But in their hearts of hearts, they knew that Kim was right.

John Maley   *1993*

THE GHOST OF LIBERACE

The pink triangle on my lapel was a gift from
Adolf. That bastard knew the power of identity.
Do you? I've concocted a plan. It's outrageous.
I'm going to appear in Sauchiehall Street,
dressed like the ghost of Liberace. I'll whistle
at workmen, I'll wink and wiggle and waltz
to Cole Porter. I'll wield a Wildean wit. I'll
rave with Jimmy Somerville's Ruchill falsetto.
The red ribbon on my lapel was a gift from
God. Or whatever angel knows the power of mercy.
Do you think through grief we'll find a voice?
Sew our names for the world to see for good?
Do you understand that silence equals death?
Click your ruby slippers and take a deep breath.

Dòmhnall Alasdair   *1994*

AN TUBA

Bha a' gheòla aig bonn nan creagan àrd a tha aig ceann shìos croit m' athar. Dh' fhàg cuideigin a sin i o chionn fhada, agus bhiodh sinne – mi fhìn agus mo bhràthair, Dòmhnall Beag – a' faighinn a mach a dh'iasgach leatha corr uair còmhla ri inbhich. 'S e an Tuba a bha aig a h-uile duine oirre. Bha mi fhìn faisg air deich bliadhna a dh' aois agus Dòmhnall Beag faisg air seachd.

Aon oidhche Shathairne rinn sinn plana a bha anabarrach dàna nar beachd fhìn – dhèidheadh sinn a mach leis an Tuba Là-na-Sàbaid. Bha soisgeulaiche ainmeil gu bhi anns a' chubainn, agus bhiodh am baile gu lèir ga èisdeachd. 'S e Iain – mo bhràthair eile a bha anns an oilthigh – a bhiodh ag ullachadh an diathad.

Nuair a dh' fhalbh ar pàrantan dhan eaglais thubhairt mi ri Iain gu robh sinn a' dol cuairt chon a' chladaich. Bha mi a' faireachdainn ciontach ag innse breug do Iain, oir bha e na sheòrsa de Dhia againn. Bha earbsa againn ann nach fhaigh mi air innse. Cha robh ceist a chuireadh sinn air nach freagradh e, chan ann mar ar pàrantan "b'e sin toil Dhè", ach le saidheans. 'S e saidheans a bha e a' dèanamh ann an oilthigh Obair Dheadhain.

Tha cuimhne agam fhathast air feadhainn de na rudan a bhiodh sinn a' foighneachd dha – "Carson a tha an t-adhar gorm?" no "Carson a tha uisge fliuch?" no "Am bheil imleag aig meanbh-chuileag?"

Ach a' mhadainn-sa bha rud nas cudhthromaiche air ar n-inntinn. "An cuir Dia daoine dhan Loch Theine airson a bhi 'g iasgach air Là-na-Sàbaid?" arsa Dòmhnall Beag.

"Cha chuir," ars Iain, a' rusgadh a' bhuntàta.

"Dè mu dheidhinn feadhainn a thèid a mach le eathar?"

"Chan eil cron sam bith ann a rud den t-seòrsa sin."

"Nach bi 'ad a' gìosgail am fiaclan ann an Ifrinn?"

Sheall Iain ris le uabhas. "De mu dheidhinn?" ars esan.

"Chan fhaigh mise air gìosgail a dhèanamh," arsa Dòmhnall Beag, a' cuir a charbad bho thaobh gu taobh.

"Coma leat," ars Iain, a' gàireachdainn, "cha bhi agad ri dhèanamh." "De tha cearr oirbh? Nach b' fheàrr dhuibh a dhol air ur cuairt?"

Bha e a' gaireachdainn. Cha do smaoinich e gu robh càil seach a' rathad air ar n-aire.

Bha a' là ciùin, grianach, blàth, agus bha am muir a staigh. Mas do chrom sinn chon a' chladaich thubhairt mi gur e mise a' sgiobair, agus cha do chuir Dòmhnall Beag an aghaidh sin idir. Chuir sinn dhinn ar brògan agus ar stocainnean agus sheas sinn aig an Tuba air chrith le sùileachas. Chuir sinn feamainn air na lunnan gus am biodh e na b' fhasa a' gheòla a ghluasad, ach cha robh seo cho duilich 's a bha dùil againn, oir bha a' leathad leinn agus am muir faisg. Ann an tiotadh bha an Tuba air bhog agus leum sinn na broinn. Mar sgiobair dh' òrdaich mi na ràimh a chuir a mach agus glè aithghèarr bha an tràigh fada air ar cùl. Dh' òrdaich mi nise na ràimh a thoirt air bòrd agus chuir sinn a mach na dubhain a bha againn air am biadhadh la faochagan. Cha robh guth an nis air eaglais no air diathad, agus nuair a sheall mi an àirde cha robh sgial air tìr.

Bha a' cheò air sgaoileadh bho thaobh a' chladaich agus cha b' fhada gus a robh sinn ann a saoghal sàmhach, dorch. Aig an aon àm mhothaich mi gu robh a' gheòla ao-dìonach. Bha a' sàl air èirigh gu ar casan rùisgte air an ùrlar, agus cha robh taoman againn. "Dè 'n taobh a tha an tràigh?" arsa Dòmhnall Beag. Cha robh fios agam. "Bu chòir fios a bhi aig a' sgiobair," ars esan. Bha sinn an uairsin le chèile sàmhach. Saoilidh mi gu robh sin mar seo air son greis mhòr agus sùilean casaideach Dhòmhaill Bhig orm. "Chan eil fios agad dè 's còir dhuinn a dhèanamh," ars esan, mu dheireadh. Ach gu h-obann chuala sinn èigheachd – guth Iain agus dh' eigh sinne cuideachd. "Tha mi dol a thighinn a mach thugaibh," ars esan. "Dèanaibh eigheachd gus a lorg mi sibh."

"Dè dh' èigheas sin?" arsa Dòmhnall Beag.

"Rud sam bith."

"Sròin a' chlamhain," arsa mise.

"Sròin Dosag," arsa Dòmhnall Beag. B'e seo nàbaidh dhuinn air a robh sròin mhòr.

Ann an ùine ghoirid chuala sinn na pluban a bha Iain a' dèanamh anns an t-sàl, agus abair gun d' fhuair sinn faochadh nuair a thàinig e air bòrd gun stiall ach a dhrathais bheag. "Nach robh sibh a' cluinntinn mac-talla nan creag?" ars esan.

"Cha do smaoinich thusa air a siud," arsa Dòmhnall Beag rium-sa.

"Tha cuideachd bonn suaile ann," ars Iain, a' tarraing gu làidir air na ràimh. "Chan fhaca duine a riamh suaile a' tighinn bho thaobh a' chladaich."

"Cha robh fios agad air a siud a bharrachd," arsa Dòmhnall

Beag, a' cuir roimhe gu nàraicheadh e mi. Cha robh dragh
agam, oir bha Iain air bòrd agus bha mi cinnteach gu robh sinn
sàbhailte. Ach nuair a dh'fhalbh eagal a' bhàis thàinig eagal eile.
"N dùil an e rabhadh dhuinn a bha 'sa cheò air son gun bhris
sinn an t-Sàbaid?" arsa mise.
    "Cha b'e. Cha robh càil ann ach tachartas."
    "Na robh sinn air ar bàthadh," arsa Dòmhnall Beag, "'n
dùil a robh sinn air faighinn a nèamh?"
    "Tha am bìoball ag ràdh gum bheil Dia mall a chum feirge
agus pailt ann an tròcair. Chan e eildear a th'ann."
    "Dh' fhàg sinn ar brògan air an tràigh," arsa Dòmhnall
Beag. "Am beil bùth bhrògan ann a nèamh?"
    "Tha a h-uile càil ann."
    "Dè mu dheidhinn appendix mo sheanar?" Bha am bodach
air tilleadh as an ospadal o chionn dà là.
    "Gheibh e tè ùr."
    "'M bheil bùth shiùcairean ann?"
    Mas d' fhuair Iain air freagairt dh' èigh mi ris gu robh mi
a' faicinn sgeirean, agus cha b' fhada gus a robh sinn air an
tràigh. Nuair a shlaod sinn an Tuba suas thubhairt Iain: "Cha
robh sibh air a suid a dhèanamh nur n-aonar."
    "Bha am muir air falbh leatha," arsa Dòmhnall Beag.
"Abair sgiobair!"
    An ath mhadainn chaidh m' athair sìos leis a' bhò gun
cheann a' chroit far am biodh i air feisde aige san t-samhradh.
Nuair a thill e thubhairt e ri Iain: "Chan eil mi faighinn lorg air
a' clach leis am bi mi bualadh bacan na bà. Nach fheuch thu a
lorg thu tè dhomh air a' chladach." Chaidh sinne còmhla ri
Iain. Bha dòchas againn gun tugadh e a mach sinn anns an
Tuba, ach nuair a sheall mi a bhroinn an eathar thàinig
tuainealaich orm. Bha toll mòr anns an t-slige aice agus clach
mhòr anns a' ghainmhich foipe. Dh'èigh sinn ri Iain agus nuair
a thàinig e sheall e an àirde. "'S ann bho bhàrr na creige a
chaidh a' clach sin a leigeil sìos," ars esan. "Cha tèid an Tuba
gu muir tuilleadh."
    "'N dùil cò rinn e?" arsa mise, cho brònach 's ged a bhithinn
air caraid a chall. Chunna mi gu robh deòir a' sileadh a sùilean
Dhòmhaill Bhig.
    "Cha bhiodh e duilich sin a lorg," ars Iain.
    "Sin a' chlach a bha aig m' athair air son a' bhacain," arsa
Dòmhnall Beag. "Tha làrach innte a rinn am bacan." Bha gal
anns a' ghuth aige.

"Tha thu dèanamh glè mhath," ars Iain.

"Tha cuideigin a' feuchainn ris a' choire a chuir air m' athair," arsa mise.

"Math dha rìribh," ars Iain. "Cha robh duine a' cleachdadh a' clach ach m' athair ach bidh làrach mheuran eile oirre a nis, oir cha robh miotagan air an eucoireach idir. Bha poll air a mheuran nuair a thog e a' clach. Cha bhiodh am poileas fada a' lorg dè na meuran a rinn na làraich. Ach ma thèid sinn chon a' phoileas lorgaidh iad làraich bhur meuran fhèin air na ràimh agus cuiridh sin an ceòl air feadh na fidhle. Cluinnidh m' athair gu robh sibh a muigh leis an Tuba air an t-Sàbaid. 'N dùil nach e bhi sàmhach mu dheidhinn seo a b' fheàrr?"

Agus sàmhach a bha sinn air son ioma bliadhna. Bha sinn le chèile anns an àrd sgoil agus ann a sgioba ball-cois mas do dh' innis mo mhàthair dhuinn gur e Iain fhèin a bhris an Tuba air a robh a leithid de ghaol againn aig an àm. Bha mo mhàthair a' coimhead rinn mar gu robh i smaoineachadh gun cuireadh a naidheachd troimhe chèile sinn. Ach rinn mise gàire, agus thubhairt Dòmhnall Beag: "Nach dòcha gur e sinn dh'fhàg beò sinn fhathast." Bha ar leanabanas seachad.

Gerry Cambridge

THE DRUNKEN LYRICIST
Orkney

We met that grey dull evening on the east shore.
Roaring round the bend he came, flat out
at fifteen miles an hour, and stopped. We had to shout
till he turned off his engine. *It's going to pour*
it looks like: me. Oa, I'm haardly cancerned
thee night wi weather, man! he said, flat cap askew.
Gap-toothed smile. Torched cheeks. Eyes' Atlantic blue.
Hiv you seen any? Weemun? Whisky burned
its golden track in him, and he would search.
's that wun, man? – the shore's dark speck.
Not waiting a reply, through the bright wreck
of that grey evening, he roared off, with a lurch.
His tractor almost reared on its back tyres.
Fifteen miles an hour flat out, parched by amber fires.

Robin Fulton *1995*

I GIVE BACK SOME BRIGHTNESS

Summer is a present tense.
I am snagged by my decades.

One more weight has been added.
It's invisible. The sun

stares at the almost-weightless
and the never-to-be-budged

and both oblige with brightness.
My present tense tries to be

translucent as a thin leaf
and opaque as a thick stone

both at once. I give back some
brightness. And hide away some.

A spider's web makes the best
of two worlds, half-hanging on

to earth, parachuting on
its fistful of half-held air.

Brent Hodgson   *1995*

from PEPYS IN MY DIARY

1. Monandaeg: Today I wrote a concrete poem.

```
            HED
       IST      AEG
    AEG                OFT
   AND                   HEM
 MON                        ONA
```

Monandaeg is the daeg of the mona.

Glossary: hed   head
           ist   Gothic spelling of the 3rd pers.
                             sing. of the verb to be
           aeg   egg
           oft   often
           hem   them
           mon   a Scotsman
           Monandaeg   Monday
           daeg   day
           mona   moon
           moon   a satellite useful for the
                             measurement of time.

At this stage I wol throwe an aeppel in the watar-werks,
and declare that concrete poetry is a queerios bisseness.
My kenning (or cunning) of the subject I wol summarize:

1. Concrete poetry, unlic the pulp of an aeppel,
   is ful of indigestiblelness.
2. An aeppel is not a compound fruht.

2. **Frigedaeg: Today I fund lippestick.**

The lippestick was pleesant to smell:
    it mynded me of the sent of freesia.   sent: scent
I titched it with my tonge and I kent it was,
    ful of moisturising emollients.
But hwaether the lippestick wolde last an efnung,
    of eeting and drinking
    withutan federing or bledan,
    I wolde ne ken.
I have bene tolde that the lippestick,
    does nat stick to cigarettes or to glasses.
Furthermore, the lippestick hadde bene applied in twa cotes,
    to lippes that were baith clene and drie.
The lippestick that I fund,
    was on the lippes of Morag.
Sche asked me nat to telle hir husbonde of hir lippestick:
    of hir lippes of efer-lasting escarlate luke;
    of hir lippes, which sche coude pout.
Sche cyssed me agane.
    Wol you telle my husbonde? said sche.
Ne, I said;
    I wol nat telle your husbonde that you dyde spend,
    £11.50 for lippestick,
    in a handy, no frills, compact container.

3. **Today I wrote a pece of fiction mysticus.**

Today my lyf as a homo sapiens cam back to me.
I can not say why; I am content being a homo novis.
God! what a strange lyf was that, being a homo sapiens.

Morning efter morning
            endless cornflakes and cuppes of tea.
Day efter day unintelligible sounds dirling
            in my eer.
Neaht efter neaht wahting
            for the robbour cumen to my door.
Yeer efter yeer
            withutan wings to flee:
            to flee ofer the hwite shore.

4. **Today I mette a gerl – alswa a pece mystikos.**

I mette a gerl today.

Hir muid as derk as the wudd.

Her loosed clathes the cullour of deid gress.

Hir earmes were sweeping in the wind.

At hir feet lay a wraeth of snaw.

5. Today I pretended to be a Tae.

I wanted to be a Ta, but a Ta is an Anglo-Saxon Toe, and who wolde believe me in Scotland if I said – I am a Ta! and so I settled for the next best thyng which was a Scottish Tae. And a Tae in Scotland is a Toe and everybuddie in Scotland kens what a Tae is.
Weel, I howp thay do and schame on thase who do not. There is not at the present as far as I am aware, any ordinance forbidding the Scottish citezein from assuming the identity of a Tae. The situation may be different in England, as it is an independent contree with its own laws.
But as ye may ken, taking on the identity of a Tae in Scotland is not a full-time occupation: Scotland does not have a national theatre in which the actour can display his or her acting skills while on the plate-forme: that is why the Scottish public rarely gets to see a buddy portraying a Tae. And so I walked barefoot in a Scottish field free of thistles. And do you ken I was lucky, because there was not any thrissels in yon field either. I walked up and doun and as I walked, I counted my Taes:

$$1 - 2 - 3 - 5 - 6$$

and the rest of thame: I forget how many exactly. I performed this exercise until voila! I became a Tae.
My uther Taes being redundant, mairched off this-a-wey and that-a-wey and eventually thay made their wey up a stane dyke to where thay had a vantage point ofer the hale field. A stane dyke is a unique feature of the Scottish landscape, and as I was only taute the Scottish language at the schule, I am sorely troubled to render to the reader of English, a precise translation of the twa words 'stane' and 'dyke'.
– And as I walked in the field, I was no longer 'me', but ane enormous Tae.
From the top of the stane dyke I coude heer the laughter of my uther Taes, and thay were laughing at me.
There was a bunch of my Taes on that stane dyke: I wolde say 2 or 3 or 5 of thame at least.
And as I jigged along I heered thame count:

$$1 - 1 - 1 - 1 - 1 - 1 \ldots$$

Richard Price   *1995*

AS, AS

What falls between us
is the rain
as thick as, as fast as,

and you're there with your ornaments
and we're here with our tucked-up nets
(say the car-park dividing us joins us),

and the snow
is just heavier than leaves,
just more liquid,
plural as millions et cetera –

it's as fluid I mean
as creamy falling stars

and what falls between us
falls and finishes the.

'Bye' I say, say,
and all of us, well, wave.

Ruaraidh MacThòmais   *1995*

IAIN GRIMBLE (1921–1995)

Nuair a thuit thu aig bun na staidhre
dh' fhairich ar n-eachdraidh an grèim;
ged a bha an rathad fada
bho Hong Kong, troimh Winchester
is Ath-nan-damh is Lunnainn,
ràinig thu Dùthaich Mhic Aoidh
is dh' fhàg thu làrach innt'
a mhaireas.
Bha do bhodhaig làidir
's do chridhe dìleas
chun na mionaid mu dheireadh,
do pheann a' freagairt d' inntinn
le leum-àrd
's do bhuille-snàmh
a' sgathadh uisgeachan buairidh
's a' fàgail soilleir ás do dhèidh.
Tha fhios gun cuir Rob Donn fàilt ort
ma thachras sibh ann a saoghal eile,
's bidh sgeulachd no dhà agaibh
mu Shrath Nabhair 's Gleann a Gallaidh.
Dhuinne, a th' air ar fàgail,
gus an tig am beum
bidh cuimhn' againn air d' uaisleachd
's air do ghàire
's air sgaiteachd do sgeul.

IAN GRIMBLE (1921–1995)

When you fell at the foot of the stair
our history felt the pain;
though it was a long road
from Hong Kong, via Winchester
and Oxford and London,
you reached the MacKay Country
and left a mark there
that will last.
Your body was strong
and your heart true
to the last minute,
your pen answering your mind
with a high-jump,
and your breast-stroke
splitting the waters of contention
and leaving clear water behind you.
Undoubtedly Rob Donn will welcome you
if you meet in another world,
and you will exchange stories
about Strath Naver and Glen Gollaidh.
For us, left here,
until the stroke comes
we will remember your nobility
and your laughter
and the cutting-edge of your story.

Rody Gorman   *1996*

NAM CHLARSAIR BALBH

Shil mi ceòl dhut air crann nan teud
Fo stiùireadh a' bhàird

'S gheàrr thu dhìom m' ìnean
'S thug thu an ceòl às mo mheòir

'S dh'fhàg thu mi nam amadan
Leam fhìn a' gabhail nan deòr.

ME AS A DUMB HARPER

I poured out music for you on the tree of strings
Under the bard's guidance

And you cut off my nails
And took the music out of my fingers

And left me a fool
On my own uttering tears.

NAM IAIN ODHAR

Bidh mi togail
Mo phìob' nam Iain Odhar
Ach an cuir a' ghleadhraich na cois
Mo chuimhn' ort mu làr

Ach air cho dùrachdach
'S gun sèid mi m' anail,
Bidh thu fhathast air mo chùlaibh
Nad dhos
Nach siubhail air falbh
Ach a chumas am fonn agam rèidh.

ME AS IAIN ODHAR

I lift up my pipe
Like Iain Odhar
So that the racket it makes
Will get rid of my memories of you

But however earnestly
I blow on with my breath
You'll still be there behind me
As a drone
That won't go away
But which keeps my trim/melody regular.

LOCH

Smaoinich!
Thusa nad loch
Agus reothadh cruaidh air uachdar
Anns an do shnàmh mi rùisgte uair.

LOCH

Just imagine!
You a loch
With a hard sheet of ice on its surface
In which I swam naked once.

DUBH

Cha drùidh mi ort fhèin
Ach nam dhubh
Nach tig am follais
Ach uair ainneamh nad fhianais
'S mi ri saothair
Gus d' ìomhaigh a chur an làthair
A-staigh ann am marbhan
Na duilleig' air do bheulaibh.

INK

I can only make an impression on you
As ink
Which only becomes visible
Very occasionally in your presence
As I labour
To present your image
In the margin
Of the page in front of you.

Donny O'Rourke   *1996*

DEAR ANDREW McGREGOR

I've become my mum –
wireless on all morning
not Wogan or Clyde
for me but Radio Three
and you Andrew McGregor,
Whose name I growl
with its gritty, rolling, Rob Roy
'Rs' a great big gruff,
hairy and heroic name,
trailing gravel and burrs –
though you yourself have mild
Tony Blair style vowels and Home
Counties headnotes: a high
nuzzling whinny that seems
to say 'Nanny, can I
have a sugar lump?'
I'd give you a sugar lump:
I'd give you two! Andrew
are you medium height,
slight, thinning in your thirties,
I know you cycle in;
you told me. Bet it's not
a mountain bike. Bet you!
I used to get up with you
at seven; now we both start
at the crack of six.
Dear Andrew, this is not
some foolish fad of mine.
My dial's spinning!
My aerial's up!
If I've guessed right about
you, send me a sign:
make your third piece on
Thursday, the misterioso
movement from Furtwangler's
pre-war recording of
Bruckner's symphony number nine.

Aonghas MacNeacail   *1997*

AN DUIBHRE BEÒ

ged is fhada bho choinnich sinn, a dhuibhre
tha thu fhathast na do chat dhomh
drùidhteach, dubh agus diamhair
na do nathair, na do luibhe

cluinneam do chrònan seòlta
caora, mas fhìor
's mar a tha thu ag èaladh
troimh dhoras dùinte mo shùilean
do dhuilleach mar neòil gun shoillse
ga mo phasgadh, ga mo phasgadh
ann an cille thruagh mo thuairmsean fhìn
agus nuair a bha mi an dùil
gun robh mo mhacmeanmhain balbh
leig thusa mach mo bhòcain

THE LIVING DARK

though it's long since I first met you, darkness
you are still a cat to me
pervasive, dark and secret
you are snake, you are weed

I hear your cunning purr
pretend to be sheep
and the way you slither
through the closed door of my eyes
your foliage like clouds without light
wrapping me, wrapping me
in the meagre cell of my own surmise
then when I have assumed
that my imagination's dumb
you release my bogeymen

Kevin MacNeil 1997

AN ACARSAID

na rionnagan a' deàrrsadh san uisge
na rionnagan a' deàrrsadh na mo chridhe
an Cuan Sgìth mar sgàthan dorch
's do phòg mu dheireadh
air mo ghruaidh fhathast
balbh, fuar, fad air falbh
mar seann ghealach
a' cuimhneachadh air acarsaid eile

THE HARBOUR

the stars shining in the water the stars
shining in my heart the Minch like a
dark mirror and your farewell kiss
still on my cheek – dumb, cold,
distant – like an old moon
remembering another harbour

John Scott MacPherson   *1997*

LEUM NAM BUFFALO

bha an duine dearg ann
an t-àm a bha sin
nuair a bhuaileadh am buffalo na raointean
le fuaim na tàirneanaich

agus bhiodh daoine a' fuireach
fad a' gheamhraidh
gus an tàinig aiteamh na gaoithe
a' *chinook* a chuir sgleò orra
gus an do thuit na beathaichean bochd
far na creige àird
a bhiodh a' toirt dhaibh
sealladh na sìorraidheachd
mionaid no dhà mus do dh'eug iad:

a' phrèiridh mhòir na sìneadh
fichead mìle air falbh
cho farsainn ris a'chuan
's gun do theab iad smaointinn
gur ann ann an cuideachd Mhaois
a bha iad
a' sgaradh a' chuain
air an t-slighe gu tìr a'gheallaidh
Eipheit-Alberta

air am buaireadh leis an fhìrinn
a' falach ann an gath na grèine
a' priobadh a-mach
air latha grianach garbh geamhraidh

agus thogadh an duine dearg
suas a shùilean
gus deò a thoirt dhan Spiorad Mhòr
'son gaoth 's grian
sgòthan 's feur
an tìr air leth
agus àm bàis
ann an uillt staoin na fala
aig bonn na creige

HEAD-SMASHED-IN-BUFFALO-JUMP

the redman was there
at that time
when buffalo would beat the great plains
with thunder sounds

and people would wait
all winter
till the wind's thaw
the chinook that muddled them
till the poor beasts fell
from off the high cliff
giving them a vision of eternity
a moment or two before death

the great prairie stretched out
twenty miles away
as far as the sea
till they almost figured
they were in the company of Moses
separating seas
on the way to the promised land
Egypt – Alberta

overcome by the truth
hiding in a sun's ray
peeking out
on a wild sunny winter day

and the redman would raise his eyes
to grant lifespark to the Great Spirit
for wind and sun
clouds and tallgrass
the land alone
and death's time
in shallow rivulets of blood
at the bottom of the cliff

Head-Smashed-In-Buffalo-Jump is a site in southern
Alberta; a cliff used by Indian buffalo hunters before
the arrival of the whiteman and the horse.

Pete Fortune   *1998*

A DEATH IN THE FAMILY

My brother is going to die. Nobody knows for sure when this
will happen (how can they?) but the consultant dealing with his
case reckons somewhere between a couple of months and a year.
This is what he told me, the end of August 1997:
   'We have the results of John's tests, and the news is not great.
He has a tumour on his left lung, and it has attached itself to sur-
rounding bone structure. This is what is causing him such pain
in his shoulder and back. A couple of ribs are actually cracked,
and we hope that radiotherapy will reduce the size of the
tumour, and alleviate the pain to an extent. That's all we can
hope to achieve though. Nobody's talking about a cure here, I
have to emphasise that. I'm afraid the outlook is pretty grim.'
   He went on to tell me that a bone scan had also revealed
what he referred to as a cluster of hot spots elsewhere, mainly
in John's left leg and arm. It seemed that cancerous growths
were on the verge of erupting there too. I'd been expecting bad
news because John had looked really unwell for some time, but
all the same, it was still a shock hearing it confirmed.
   'How long do you think he has?' I asked.
   'Difficult to say,' he replied. 'The sort of tumour he has
tends to be slow-growing, but if it moves into the centre of his
chest I'd expect him to deteriorate rapidly. It could be a couple
of months, it could be a year. The quality of life remaining is
what concerns us now though. I can assure you, we will see to
it that he is kept as comfortable as possible.'
   Actually, my brother died twelve years ago, but they got him
going again. He fell down a flight of stairs and lay undiscovered
for around eight hours. He developed a blood clot on the brain,
and by the time someone discovered him he was in a pretty bad
way. I got a phone call to say he was in hospital suffering from
concussion.
   When I arrived at the hospital they gave it to me straight.
'We need to transfer him to the Southern General in Glasgow
for specialist treatment, or he's going to die. Trouble is, if we
attempt to move him right now, there's every likelihood that
he'll die.' I said to move him, and they did. And he lived.
   John was in a coma for a couple of weeks, and in hospital for
months, but live he did, despite the fact that his heart actually

stopped beating a couple of times. He emerged a different person though, 'head injured' the euphemism, brain damaged the fact of the matter. His basic intelligence was intact, but the most disturbing thing was the fairly profound personality change which had taken place. At times it was as if another human being had been implanted in my brother's body. He seemed generally 'odd' too. It sounds cruel but it's true because I heard people say so – *he's kind of odd now.*

But he eventually returned to the community, living alone in his flat (he'd gone through a divorce just before his accident) and generally muddling along. He got by, just. I can see in retrospect that he needed more support than he ever got – especially from me – but to indulge in an outpouring of guilt would be an attempt to exorcise it, and I'm not about to go into that.

So my brother had a go at dying once before, and now here he is again. This time the consultant seems pretty certain he *will* die – just a matter of when. Never once did the consultant mention the word cancer to me – tumour was the most direct reference he made, along with a host of other terms which later had me fumbling through the dictionary. Maybe if he'd used the word cancer to John, the message might have got through. He said he'd told my brother he had a tumour and that they were going to attempt treating it with radiotherapy – they'd just have to wait and see. He'd left it at that, hoping the rest would be deduced.

John told me he had a tumour, but that there was nothing to worry about, it was benign and they were going to zap it with radiotherapy. The worst that could happen was that he'd maybe go bald. He said being bald at 52 was no big deal. He said things could have turned out a whole lot worse. He smiled as he said so.

I spoke to his GP about the situation. I'd been in recent contact with him, because we were both concerned about John's living conditions. His head injury had left him negligent when it came to hygiene issues, and the mess he'd been living in amounted to self-neglect. I told the GP about my brother's confusion regarding his diagnosis and prognosis. I presumed it was down to his head injury. The doc reckoned not necessarily so, said it could be a classic case of denial. He saw it all the time, said many terminally ill people just put the shutters up when told of their fate, just completely blocked out the facts and constructed an alternative reality. He said it was best I just go along with it, let John dictate the pace. 'Who are you,' he said, 'to deny him his denial?'

So I do go along with it, wondering each visiting hour how things will be. There's friends and relatives visiting who John hasn't seen in a long time – I wonder if that doesn't tell him that something serious is going on. There's the chance too that one of them will be verbally explicit, confront him with his fate. Sometimes too I wonder if he *does* fully understand, but is maybe trying to protect me, and I'm going along with the pretence, trying to protect him. A weird kind of cat and mouse game, perhaps?

Once the news had properly sunk in I became briefly obsessed with the whole business of cancer, became convinced for a while that I had it – *that everyone I loved had it.* Then I grew curious and sought out the textbooks in the library. I learned some really gory things about cancer, but managed to divorce those terrible things from the illness my brother was suffering. Maybe I was into a kind of denial too?

Anyway, I learned that quite often a tumour will resemble the host body. That is to say, a kidney tumour may well be made up of – in effect – another kidney, gone kind of haywire. Or the tumour may *not* resemble the host body at all. Tumours for example can grow hair, or even have teeth. Having teeth seemed the worst thing of all, the thought of this thing growing inside you – *with teeth.* It seemed so symbolically apt in a very macabre sort of way. It made me realise why medical people have to so often resort to euphemism.

I forced myself away from the textbooks. Morbid. Besides, there were practical issues to deal with. John hasn't worked since his head injury, had been on jobseeker's allowance. I don't think he could ever have held down a job again, but that's academic. He's certainly not fit to work now, so he had to be transferred across to another benefit, to incapacity benefit. I handled all the paperwork for him, four books – not forms – *books of forms*, all of which asked for pretty much the same information. My head still reeling from the fact that my brother's dying, but the state demands that all this paperwork be dealt with, and at the end of the day he'll still receive exactly the same amount of (meagre) money in benefits.

A week after I'd filled in all those forms, a matching set was sent to the hospital for John to fill in. No one knows what happened to the ones I filled in, and nobody knows either when he's likely to receive any money. Nobody seems to really care. All the young women I've dealt with seem polite and very charming, but quite unable to supply anything approaching useful information. The caring state under New Labour.

The state's going to have to play another role too. Once released from hospital, John's going to need home help, meals on wheels, nurses to call in and check on medication, etc., all that kind of business. A medical social worker is organising this side of things, and I'm working in liaison with her. At times it seems as if my whole life has been hijacked to help organise what's left of my brother's. I'm not complaining about this, how can I? If that's not what brothers are for, then what exactly is it they're meant to be for?

So as I write he's still in hospital, and we're still waiting for the care package to fall into place. Last night when I visited him he was talking again about what he was going to do once he was better. I can never look him in the eye when he talks that way, like the whole pretence has stripped away any honesty that exists in our relationship. But he's entitled to his denial. It's maybe the last thing he has. But all the same, I think, he must know what's going on. Somewhere, deep deep down, he *must* know. Or is the human psyche really capable of such a massive deception? Will he just grow weaker and weaker, all muddled up with drugs and just slip away? Without properly knowing?

He phoned me there. Just as I finished typing that paragraph the phone rang and it was him phoning from hospital. From the portable public phone they can wheel alongside your bed, where sometimes the nurses just stand and listen to the conversation. They do – some of them – I've seen them. Anyway he phoned, and he needs me to bring some matches or a lighter when I visit later on. He's clean out and he's desperate. He's in hospital dying of lung cancer and still he smokes about forty a day. Two lethal cuts of hand-rolling stuff – which he mixes together – and then puff puff puffs in this smelly little smoking room he has access to. What the hell. What's the point in him stopping now? But anyway he phoned and that's good because it's like he gets to put in a live appearance here. Yes, that's good. That's defiance for you.

I appreciate defiance. Death's been big news of late, the death of someone we were encouraged to see as defiant. While my brother's illness was revealing itself up there on the Bankend Road, Diana, Princess of Wales – scourge of the royal establishment – got herself killed. By all accounts the driver was well over the legal alcohol limit, as well as having a cocktail of drugs flowing through him, and on top of it all it seems he was doing well over the ton. Response? Blame the boys on the scooters. I suppose such a ridiculous response amounts to a kind of defiance too.

The mass hysteria her death generated I would have found hard enough to take at any time, but for it to coincide with my brother's news was lousy timing. Sometimes it made me angry, and I wanted to go and kick the bunches of flowers dumped around Queensberry Square. Chase away all the silly old women reading the messages on the cards. But the whole thing was weird. Really, really weird. It was like grief manifesting itself as a human *desire*. All those people seemed to *want* something to be sad about. I can only figure they must have uneventful lives. Diana's seemed a kind of glamorous death, with loads of romantic ingredients mixed in. Maybe that was the attraction. But real death's not like that.

I see real death almost every night I'm up at the hospital visiting my brother. Real death's catching a glimpse of a little old man all hunched up in bed, face invisible beneath an oxygen mask, scrawny little rib cage going ten to the dozen. Real death's seeing his wife sitting bearing witness to it all, his grown-up sons not knowing what to do or say, of maybe wanting to – but being too embarrassed to – put their arms around their old mum.

Real death is my brother waiting to happen. Real death is why I'm writing this: I suppose it might seem to some people a kind of brutal and cold-hearted response to my brother's death. Or at least the death I'm told can't be far away. But I don't know why I'm writing about it. I'm a writer of sorts, and I suppose it's what writers do. We write about things. It's probably never done any writer – or anybody in the world – much good, even if we like to kid ourselves on from time to time that it does. *It's art. Others might find benefit. There is a universal truth.* All that kind of nonsense. But I don't know what the hell I can do and so I find myself doing this, and feeling tacky and manipulative in the process.

And so to the end – sometimes in my stories I have difficulties with endings. This piece has a natural ending – still to come – and no one knows for sure when that will be. Being a fiction writer, I know that some people speculate as to what's real and what's made up in my stories. No one need do that with this piece. This is the real thing – and it's grim.

This is what they mean by dirty realism.

John Fortune died on 30th October 1997
R.I.P. Brother

Norman Kreitman   *1998*

THE EXTRA

'I'll say this only once,' said the director,
massaging his temples.
'You're gangsters, see, very tough, sitting around
drinking in this bar.
Charlie here runs in with a warning.
You all leap up
and run out after him. Two takes only,
and no cock-ups.
After that you get your money.'

Later, idling towards my room,
panning past billboards
losing their skins, drifting through the longshot
of the market at night
as a different life emerged from the shadows,
I appreciated the warmth
in my wallet, and felt grateful to that man
who explained things
so clearly, that for two whole minutes
I understood the plot.

Meg Bateman

AIR TILLEADH DHACHAIGH

'S fheàrr dùsgadh tron oidhche le casan beaga air a' chluasaig
na cadal gun bhriseadh ann an taigh-òsda uasal,
teilibhisean am falach ann am preasa mahogany,
bòrd-sgrìobhaidh san uinneig fo chùirtearan cosgail;
b' fheàrr m' fhuil ùr air an searbhaidearan sneachdaidh
is trod nan caileagan ann an taigh-nighe ceathach,
na lainnir nan rùmannan a bheireadh a' chreids' ort
gur duine eile an àite eile aig àm eile thu ...
'S fheàrr mo chaithris a-nochd fo ghealaich air chuthach,
's mo bheatha dol seachad gun fhianais, gun fhaochadh,
ceum m' athar a' dìosgail far nach eil e air an staidhre,
na taibhsean gun tuigsinn ag aomadh thar na leapa;
's fheàrr na an sògh, am bas-bhualadh 's an labhairt,
mo shlacaireachd leis gach crois, gach imcheist is bacadh
is làmhan a' phàidse mum thimcheall nan crios-teasairginn,
gus an gluais an latha gu feum 's gu misneachd mi.

HOME AGAIN

Better being woken through the night by little legs on the pillow,
than unbroken sleep in a plush hotel,
a television hiding in a mahogany chest,
a bureau in the window under expensive curtains;
better my bright blood on their snowy towels
and the scolding of the girls in a steamy laundry
than the gleam of those rooms that would have you believe
you were another person in another age ...
Better my sleeplessness under a raving moon,
with my life relentlessly passing by without witness,
my father's step where he is not on the stair,
the uncomprehending ghosts bending over the bed;
better than the luxury, applause, talk,
my buffeting by every obstacle, doubt, complexity,
with the child's arms, a safety belt, around me,
till day moves me to usefulness and courage.

David Cunningham   *1999*

DE MORTUIS

My father and I never really talked, at least not until he died; after he died he wouldn't shut up.

I wasn't there when he died. I was working in the local newsagent. I had left school and was half way through what was widely referred to as my 'gap year'. Since I had no idea what I wanted to do next this seemed a rather optimistic description of it. It felt more chasmal than gap-like to me.

I'd like to be able to say that I sensed him going, that as I walked home for lunch along the promenade I felt a part of myself being irretrievably lost. But I didn't.

Before leaving the promenade I stepped onto the sea wall for a moment. The ocean heaved and thrashed, as if fulminating against the obdurate stillness of the land. The wind, a heady mixture of salt-spray and liberated ozone, streamed through my hair and filled me with a fleeting sense of elation.

You'll catch your death standing there, he said.

It was then I knew he had gone.

When I got back to the flat I discovered I was right. Our front room, with its broad view of the Firth of Clyde, was sparsely populated by mismatched figures – my mother, my aunt, the doctor, a district nurse – like a chess board on which a draw should long ago have been declared. They all clutched steaming mugs and gazed out of the windows, as if immobilised by the mesmeric power of the storm. Barely noticed, I slipped past them and went into his room.

He lay in bed on his side. His face was a picture of repose, no longer contorted by the pain of bed sores or the emetic effects of too many drugs.

I bade him a tentative farewell in my thoughts. It was more a vague gesture than anything articulate, but he seemed to understand.

I'm still here you know. You're not getting rid of me that easily.

His voice resounded inside my head, penetrating and unignorable. I tried to stay calm and not to yield to my first instinct, which was to run from the room.

'Are you … ?'

As a doornail.
'Oh ... so how does it feel?'
It's bearable, though I can't seem to see very much. Have
they gone?
'The others? Yes.'
Thank Christ for that. Your aunt was trying to coax some
kind of death-bed repentance out of me, getting me to say that
I was ready to make peace with everyone ...
'And are you?'
The hell I am. You tell her that.
'How can I? You're supposed to be dead.'
Oh I am dead, son. I most certainly am.

That was our first conversation and, for a while, I hoped it
would be our last. But he remained a tirelessly voluble presence
inside my head over the next few days.

They passed quickly in a tumult of wind, rain and hasty
funeral preparations. Friends and neighbours arrived bearing
flowers: freesias, carnations, white lilies, even a tuberose. The
flowers were distributed around the flat and filled it with a
cloying scent that hung like anaesthetic.

His brothers – to whom he didn't speak after an obscure
argument about the division of their mother's property –
turned up one by one to condole awkwardly with us.

Probably want to stick a pin in me to make sure I'm dead.

'It's so foolish that we never talked all those years. But I suppose those sorts of things happen in families,' said his tweedy
eldest brother – a solicitor in Galloway – perched on the edge
of our sofa.

My mother and I stared numbly into our cups, hollow-eyed
from lack of sleep and all the arrivals and departures through-
out the day. We murmured vague assent.

So does incest and fratricide. But that doesn't excuse them.
'I mean I did try to get on with him when we were younger.'
All you ever got on was my nerves.
'Only we were never really interested in the same things.'
On the contrary, we were both interested in ourselves.
Snorting, I stood up and excused myself in a strangulated
voice.

'He's upset,' I heard my mother saying as I left the room.

With my aunt he was gentler, but still mocking. Towards my
mother he seemed ambivalent.

At forty-four she was tall and still slim, with the grey
hardly visible in her fine blond hair. Theirs had never – as far
as I could remember – been an especially happy marriage. A
civil engineer, he had worked abroad, in the Far East, a good
deal when I was younger. Even when he returned permanently
an emotional distance between them persisted. They shared
the same bedroom but slept in single beds. I noticed that even
before I understood what it meant. As I grew older there was
a pervading atmosphere of indifference in the flat. But, for my
sake, they managed to avoid confrontation, more or less.

When he fell ill she devoted herself to his care and their
intimacy seemed to be renewed. But now he treated all her
remarks with mordant irony, particularly if they referred to her
relationship with me.

At such times I wished I could stop up my ears against him.
True, I was close to my mother – much closer than to him – but
only because he had been absent for so large a part of my childhood. His constant insinuations that she was possessive were
like a impugning tide, eroding the foundations on which my life
was based. I resented them all the more because, at times, I had
suspected her myself.

But his most extraordinary comments were reserved for Alison.
Soulful, short-sighted Alison was my friend from school.
Walking home from our sixth-year English class, we used to talk
about our favourite writers. She was the only person I knew
who found books sexy the way most people our age found
music sexy. I found her sexy, but she went out with someone
else. I avoided referring to him when we talked. So, I noticed,
did she. I wasn't altogether surprised when they split up.

Then Dad fell ill. Though I told her and thought she was
sympathetic, I feared that turning any of her supportive hugs
into a more intimate embrace would shatter what illusions she
might cherish about me as a sensitive literary type.

I phoned her the day he died. She came over the day after
that and we went for a walk along the beach. The wind
continued to blow but the rain had eased and the impenetrable
knot of cloud had loosened slightly, admitting short bursts of
sunlight which fell on the turbid green ocean and the tousled
marram grass. When we returned from our walk we carried on

talking in the front room.

'Will you and your mother be able to stay here?' asked Alison, squinting at me.

'Probably not.'

'How's she coping?'

Struggling to contain her relief at my untimely demise.

'Pretty well. I think she feels a little bit guilty that they weren't closer in the last few years. I think perhaps she wonders if she could have tried harder.'

Ha!

Alison nodded. She knew about the problems in their marriage. Her own parents were separated.

'Well, she must be glad at least that you're still around.'

I always felt vaguely ashamed when Alison referred to my relationship with my mother, as if the fact that we had a relationship at all reflected discredit upon us both and made me ineligible as a lover.

'I suppose she is.'

'Will you go away to college at all now?'

'I don't see why not.'

'No, I only meant that she'll be on her own now if you do. And in a strange house probably. Unless of course she meets someone else.'

I shrugged. It had never occurred to me that she might meet someone else. Now that she was a widow I imagined her future as solitary and celibate: a small semi and a small car, a part-time job, female friends and aqua aerobics. There was silence while Alison and I pondered the implications of what she had said.

She's a very attractive girl you know.

'Thank you. I am aware of that.'

Don't be so defensive. I just wondered if you'd noticed.

'I'm not being defensive and yes I had noticed.'

So why haven't you done anything about it?

'Well it's complicated. I mean we're friends.'

It's not complicated. It's simple.

'Look, can't you give us some privacy. Close your eyes?'

I don't have eyes, son, I'm dead. Sans eyes, sans teeth.

'Well can't you do anything?'

No, I can't do anything. Not any more. But you can. And I'd want to fuck that girl if I were you.

'Dad!' I exclaimed, aloud this time.

Startled from her reverie, Alison looked up. I stared back at her, open mouthed. Then, in a sublime gesture of misinterpretation, she hastened to my side and put her arms around me. I held her close for longer than I had ever allowed myself to before. She felt tender and pliant as a sapling.

'It's OK,' she murmured.

I could think of nothing to say, but mumbled into her shoulder in a tone which betokened distress.

He chuckled.

Don't say I never do anything for you.

The funeral may be briefly described. It took place in weather so foul that it was hastened through by all those concerned – apart from my dad obviously – with an eagerness just short of disrespectful. While the chiaroscuro of sunshine and shower persisted, around the graveside umbrellas congregated tightly, like a cluster of toadstools.

Look at them, he said. *Can't wait to get it over with.*

'It's freezing,' I pointed out.

The coffin sat on planks of wood, laid breadthwise across the grave. I, my aunt and two of my uncles were called over to manage its final descent. I grasped a cord. The rain drummed on the lid, like bored fingertips.

The planks were slid away and the sudden weight, evenly distributed between the four of us, was arresting.

It's all right. Take the strain, he said.

I took the strain. The grave gaped obscenely, a black slot in the earth. The coffin lurched downwards into it. Just before it was swallowed up the sunlight burst upon it and created a sparkling aureole around the lid.

Isn't that beautiful? If I had eyes I could weep.

Afterwards everyone reconvened damply in our front room. The greater his relatives' estrangement from him had been, the more stridently they expressed their sense of loss. I passed amongst them with pots of tea and coffee. As I did so he dished the dirt on each person: how she had slept with her sister's husband, how he had nearly been caught for tax evasion, how they had an unhealthy attachment to their dog.

Finally it was too much for me and I fled the room. The doctor, who had come along, prescribed a sedative. (My mother had already been given one.) I was fed a huge volume of warm milk and packed off to bed.

The soporific effect of the pills was counteracted by the ache of my over-full bladder and, late at night, when they had all gone, I stumbled woozily up the hall to the bathroom and thence to the dark front room.

The windows of the flat below threw squares of light onto the lawn. The tide had retreated from the glossy ridges of sand, but the wind continued to howl.

Enjoy it while you can.

'You're still there? I was wondering.'

Yes, I'm still here. Just. I want to tell you before I go how I feel about you.

'How do you feel about me?' I asked, genuinely curious. He had offered few clues on this topic during his life.

I love you – you know that.

'Do I?'

Look, I'm trying to make amends here. I know you feel there was a distance between us when you were younger because I was never interested in who you were.

'There was a distance between us because you were in Malaysia.'

Granted. But I was in Malaysia because I loved my work and wanted to do well. Not because I didn't love you, whatever your mother might have told you.

'She never ...'

No, she never said it outright. But every time I came back I was more of an intruder between you and her. I abandoned her – so she thought – just like her father did. So you became her mainstay, her company. When I came back there wasn't a role for me any more. I know it was mostly my fault. But now that I'm gone it's going to get worse if you don't get away.

'You can't just ...'

You can't be her crutch. You've been patted on the head today for being a good son by people who haven't given a moment's thought to what will happen to you now. They've probably made you feel like you're a man. But you're not. You're still a boy, scared of the big, bad world. So you'll use the fact that she needs you to stay at home. But she's not your responsibility. She's an adult. She's her own responsibility. And you're allowing yourself to be smothered by her. You know you are. Don't tell me I'm wrong.

I squirmed, covered in a hot pelt of embarrassment, but he was relentless.

What about that girl?
'Alison.'
Alison, yes. Don't you want her?
'But we're just friends ...'
Don't make excuses.
I put my hands over my ears.
You can't shut me out, son. Of course you love your mother. She's kind and gentle and intelligent and she's always been there when you've needed her – unlike me. But she'll cut your balls off if you let her and the trouble it'll store up for both of you later won't be worth living for. You'll wake up one morning in ten years' time and realise that you've forfeited your life. And then you'll hate and resent her and she won't be able to understand why.

In a frenzy – but still disoriented from the pills – I began to unlock all the windows to drown him out. I wrenched them open one by one, admitting a ferocious wind that grew stronger by degrees. Photographs, many sepia tinted (unearthed by my mother that morning), spun through the air like so many autumn leaves. Lamp-shades spun and tilted crazily. Plants toppled, spilling soil over the carpet. The shouting pungency of the ocean filled the room.

At that moment my mother, hair streaming, entered the room. She found me standing motionless in the middle of the darkened floor. With her silk-print robe drawn round her and the wind plucking at the hem of her night-dress, she looked like an insomniac Lady of Shallott. Somewhere in the recesses of the flat a door was slammed heavily by the hurtling air.

'David, what's going on?' she asked, not unreasonably.

There was nothing I could tell her, nothing I could explain. I closed the windows and the chaos subsided. Together we tidied the room. Though she asked me again several times what was wrong, all I could say was, 'I'm sorry.' She said we would talk in the morning.

We did talk in the morning. But now that he had put all my vague apprehensions of her neediness into words I found it impossible to be honest with her. My natural impulse was to reach out to her in her perplexity. But I felt an equally strong impulse to recoil from her. So I tried to hold myself aloof.

The storm had blown itself out, my aunt had left and an uncertain silence prevailed in the flat.

In the afternoon, as we were sorting through his clothes, my mother said: 'I hope you don't feel in some way you have to be responsible for me now.'

At first I thought he was using her to perform some perverse act of ventriloquism. But as she continued I realised that these were her words:

'I've lost my husband. Whatever went wrong between us in the last few years it's still terribly sad and I'll miss him very much. But you've lost your father, and that's much worse. Life's so much harder when you don't have a father to support you and help you along. And that's all the more reason why you have to be able to enjoy your life and do what you really want with it, regardless of how I feel. You're my son. I don't expect you to be my surrogate husband as well.'

'But that means you'll be alone,' I said.

She smiled sadly.

'Darling, I've been alone for some time now. I'm used to it.'

I nodded.

'Did you hear that?' I asked him.

Yes. Yes I heard.

She went out that evening to visit a neighbour and Alison came over. We shared a bottle of red wine left over from the day before. In my room I talked about myself and about us and told her what my mother had said. She listened and sipped her wine, gazing at me over the rim of her glass. I confessed all my fears, though not that it was my dead father who had given voice to them. The wine I drank, and my exponentially increasing frankness, closed the brief distance between us. I must admit I used her sympathy as leverage in easing her towards my bed. But when she folded herself against me and I melted into her none of that – or anything else – seemed to matter.

Later we clung together. It was dark, and so quiet that I could hear my pulse. But there was a vacancy in the darkness too.

'Are you still there?' I asked.

There was no reply.

Anne Donovan   *1999*

A CHITTERIN BITE

We'd go tae the baths every Saturday mornin, Agnes and me.
Ah'd watch fae the windae, alang the grey, gluthery street, till
ah caught the first glimpse of her red raincoat and blue pixie
hat turnin the corner, then ah'd grab ma cossie, wrap it up in
the bluegrey towel, washed too many times, and heid for the
door.
Ah'm away, Mammy.
Ma mammy would appear fae the kitchen, haudin a wee
bundle, wrapped up in the waxed paper fae the end of the loaf.
Here you are, hen, your chitterin bite.
Inside were two jammy pieces, wan for me and wan for
Agnes, tae eat efter the swimmin on the way alang the road, a
chitterin bite, no enough tae fill your belly, just somethin tae
stave aff the chitterin cauld when you come oot the baths.

The noise hits you the minute you open that big green door;
the ceilin high and pointy like a chapel roof, makin everythin
echo roon its beams. It leaks, so drips of watter plash on your
heid while you're swimmin. The place is fulla weans, screechin
at their pals ower the racket. Two boys are leppin in fae the
side till big Alex blaws his whistle and threatens tae pap them
oot. There's a row a boxes at each side of the pool, the hauf
doors painted bright blue, the left-haun side for the women
and the right for the men. Agnes and me get changed in the
wan cubicle; her cossie has blue ruched bits aw roon, while
mines is yella wi pink flooers. You can just see the two wee
bumps startin tae grow on her chist and she footers aboot,
sortin her straps tae try tae cover them.
Whit dae they feel like?
You can touch them if you want.
Ah push two fingers gently intae her left breist which goes
in a wee bit under the pressure.
Is it sore?
Naw, disnae feel like anythin really.
Ah look doon at ma ain chist, totally flat. Ma mammy says
ah'll be next but ah cannae imagine it.
C'mon, let's get a move on, ah'm freezin.
We run oot the cubicle and plunk straight intae the watter,

the shock of the cauld makin us scream as usual. Ah hate jumpin intae the baths but ah love it as well.

I still go swimming, but now to the warm and brightly lit leisure centre with its saunas and steam rooms, aromatherapy massages and hot showers. Tuesday is Ladies Night and I drive there in my car; shampoo, conditioner and body lotion neatly tucked in my designer sportsbag along with a change of clothing. Dressed-up clothing; short skirt, sheer tights and silky shirt.

Afterwards I meet Matthew in the Italian restaurant, an anonymous place tucked away in a side street. We are unlikely to be spotted here for there are several places with cheaper food and more atmosphere in the area, so Matthew and I have made it our own. As I push open the door I see he is sitting at our usual table, his head bent over the menu, dark shiny hair neatly slicked back with gel. He looks up as I cross the room and I feel my breath catch in my throat.

He goes to the gym on Tuesdays before he comes to meet me so we're both showered, powdered and squeaky clean. I breathe in the sweet scent of his aftershave and the clean soapy smells of his body. His lips graze my cheek but I am aware that his eyes scan the room, just in case anyone is watching. I sit opposite him, feeling the thick white tablecloth under my hands, knowing we both look good in the pinkish glow of the candlelight. I finger the heavy wine glass, rolling the stem between my thumb and index finger, sipping delicately.

The cauld hits you as soon as you're ootside, efter the heavy door sclaffs shut. Oor hair is soakin, plastered tae wer heids and wee dreeps run doon the back of yer neck. Ma mammy says put your pixie on efter the swimmin or you'll get a cauld in the heid, but that just makes it worse, the damp seeps through tae you feel your brain's frozen up inside. Agnes and me walk, airms linked, stuffin dauds a breid intae wer mooths. Ma mammy saves us the big thick enders that you sink yer teeth intae, the raspberry jam runnin oot and tricklin doon yer chin. Ah wipe it away wi the endy the damp towel.

The cafe is two streets away. The windaes are aye steamed up so you cannae see in and the name, *Bellini's*, is printed above the door in fancy red letters. As you push open the heavy doors, heat whaps you that hard it's like bein slapped roon the face, and yer heid starts tae tingle. The cafe is divided up intae booths, each wi gless panels, frosted like sugar icing, so when you're inside wan you feel you're in yer ain wee world. The seats flip up and doon on creaky metal hinges and you have tae watch or you catch yer fingers in them. No that Agnes and me sit in the booths very often. We hardly ever have enough money for a sit-in. Usually we just get a cone or a bag of sweeties. But in the winter the smell of chips and the steam risin fae the frothy coffee makes your belly feel that empty.

Agnes and me pool wer money, leavin aside what we need tae get intae the pictures.

What'll we get – midget gems?
We got them last week – whit aboot cherry lips?
Aye, quarter a cherry lips, please.

Cherry lips are ma favourites: they're harder than midget gems but wi a funny taste tae them, wersh almost, no like any other sweeties. But the best thing is their shape; they're like wee smiley mooths aboot an inch wide an if you sook in yer ain lips and stick a cherry wan on tap it looks dead funny. Sometimes me n Agnes dae that an kid on we're kissin, just like at the pictures. Agnes crosses her eyes and makes me laugh and the cherry lips fall oot.

Affairs have their own rules, unspoken, unwritten, which soon become engraved on your heart.

1. Never go anywhere you are likely to be seen together.
2. Never show affection in public.
3. Never mention his wife.
4. Never cry.
5. Never phone him at home.
6. Never give your name if you phone him at work.
7. Never whinge if he has to cancel a meeting.
8. Never tell your friends about him.
9. Never leave marks on him.

It would be more satisfying if there were ten rules but I can't think of another.

I just broke the last rule. I can see the purply red mark, about an inch across, nestling just above his left shoulder blade, where he won't see it, but she will. I didn't do it deliberately, but what does that mean? I knew I was sooking a wee bit harder than I usually do, for a wee bit longer, yes. I wasn't really sinking my teeth into him with force, I couldn't tell it was going to leave a mark, not for sure. Guilty or not guilty? I lean, propped up on my elbow, and watch him, sleeping, lying on his right side, dark whispers of hair fanning across the white sheets, like an ad for some expensive perfume. Soon he will wake and I will watch him putting on his clothes which now lie neatly over the chair, he will kiss me without looking into my eyes and I will close the door on him and stand, listening as his footsteps echo down the hallway.

We go tae the pictures every week efter the swimmin, scramblin tae get the chummy seats up the back, sharin wer sweeties, grabbin each other's airms at the scary bits and gigglin at the love scenes. Then wan week, when we're walkin alang the road efter the baths, Agnes says:

Ah said we'd meet Jimmy McKeown and his pal at the pictures.

What?

He wants tae go wi me. He says he'll bring his pal for you.

Do you want tae go wi him?

Ah don't know, ah'll gie it a try.

Ah unlinked ma airm fae Agnes's and marched on, starin ahead.

Well you don't need me tae come too.

Agnes caught up wi me, grabbin at ma airm.

Ah canny go masel.

How no?

Ah just canny. Anyway, he's bringin his pal. If you don't go ah canny go, come on, Mary, be a pal.

The boys are waitin for us inside the foyer of the picture hoose. Jimmy McKeown is a year aulder than us, wi a broad nose, a bit bent tae the side, and straight dirty-fair hair in a side shed. The pal is staunin hauf behind him, a wee skinny laddie wi roond baby cheeks and red lips like a lassie.

This is Shuggie, he's ma cousin.

This is Mary.

Hiya.

Will we go in?

After youse, girls.

They're polite, even though Jimmy is actin the big shot and the pal still hasny opened his mooth. Agnes and me go first, intae the daurk picture hoose, Agnes leadin the way tae the back row where the chummy seats are. She sits doon in wan but when ah go tae sit next tae her she mutters *Naw, you huvty sit wi Shuggie* and shoves me ower tae the next seat, where the airm rest forms a barrier between me and her. Ah feel Shuggie's knees pushin intae mines as he squeezes by me tae sit in the other hauf of the seat. Ah move as far ower tae the side nearest Agnes that ah can, but ah canny help smellin the rough hairy smell of his sports jaicket under the sourness of the aftershave he must of plastered on his baby cheeks.

I don't expect the phone call. Not so soon anyway, not at work, not at ten o'clock in the morning, sitting at my bright shiny desk with my red folder in front of me and my bright shiny, perfectly modulated work voice:

Good morning, Mary Henderson speaking, how may I help you?

Mary? It's me, Matthew, listen, I've got to talk to you, it's urgent. Can you meet me for lunch?

Of course.

Look, I can't talk now. Can you meet me, in Sarti's? One o'clock?

OK. Make it quarter to though, you know how busy it gets there.

Right. See you then.

*

At lunchtime Sarti's is full of people in suits from nearby offices and the atmosphere is warm and faintly smoky. We sit down at a table just opposite the deli counter, which is piled high with different kinds of *panettone*. Matthew looks immaculate in his grey suit and silk floral tie, but as he bends his head to look at the menu I see a few stray bristly hairs, just where his cheekbone joins his neck, which he must have missed when shaving this morning. He looks at the menu as he speaks.

What are you having?

Spaghetti vongole, I think. I'm starving. Maybe a night of passion makes you hungry.

He looks up but does not smile.

I don't have time for lunch, I think I'll just have coffee and a bit of cake.

A chitterin bite.

What?

It's what we used to call a bite to eat, not a full meal, just enough to keep the cold out after the swimming.

He folds the menu up and replaces it in its holder.
Speaking of bites ...
I look him straight in the eyes.
Mary, do you know what kind of a mark you left on me last night?
Did I?
He squeezes his left hand tight into a fist, then releases it, repeating the movement several times as though it were an exercise.
She went berserk when she saw it.
What did you tell her?
I must have bruised myself at the gym, crap like that. How the hell do you bruise yourself on the shoulder blade? I'm sure she doesn't believe me but I think she's accepted it.
That's good.
For heaven's sake couldn't you be more careful?
Must have been carried away by passion I suppose.
You don't seem to be all that concerned about it.
I'm not the one that's cheating on my wife.

We never spoke aboot it, Agnes and me, though as the week progressed a cauldness grew between us, a damp seepin cauld like the wan that gets intae your bones when you don't dry yourself quick enough efter the swimmin. And the next Saturday, when ah haunded her her piece and jam, she shook her heid and looked away fae me.
Naw thanks, Mary, ah said ah'd meet Jimmy at Bellini's and we're gonny have chips.
Oh.
She put her airm in mines.
You can come too. It'll be good tae get sumpn hot inside us steidy just a chitterin bite. We'll go tae the pictures efter. Shuggie's no gonny be there, it's OK.
Ah pulled ma airm free of Agnes's.
Two's company, three's a crowd. Ah'll see you at school on Monday.
The sky was heavy and grey and fulla rain. Ah didnae want tae go hame but ah couldny think of where else tae go so ah wandered roon the streets, gettin mair and mair droukit, no really payin any heed tae where ah was goin, till ah fund masel ootside Bellini's. Ah cooried doon in a close on the other side of the street and watched the door till ah seen them come oot.

Agnes was laughin as Jimmy held the door open for her. Their faces were pink wi the heat and Agnes's hair had dried noo, intae wee fuzzy curls aw ower her heid. They set aff towards the pictures, him cairryin her towel under his airm. Ah unwrapped ma piece and took a bite. The breid was hard and doughy and as ah chewed it didny seem tae saften, so the big lumps stuck in ma throat. Ah stood up and heided for hame. As ah passed the waste grund on the corner, ah flung the pieces tae the birds.

I'm sorry, Mary, I think it would be better if we didn't see each other for a while.

A while?

She's going to be suspicious, she'll be watching my every move at the moment. If we wait a few weeks she'll calm down and then we can go back to where we were.

Which is?

I thought we both knew the score.

How could I have fallen in love with someone who uses expressions like that, like something out of a bad song. But I had.

Mary, you know I love you, I really do, but I can't leave her and the kids. I've never pretended I could. What we have together is very precious to me, but if it's not enough for you ...

Someone opened the door behind us and a cold draught cut through the heat of the restaurant. I looked across at Matthew, so beautiful in his perfect suit, and shook my head.

No, it's not enough. You're right. We have to end it.

I'm sorry.

So am I.

The waitress arrived with Matthew's coffee and piece of *panettone.* He looked at it for a moment, then at me.

Look, I'm sorry, I don't think I can face this. Do you mind?

No, it's OK, on you go.

He reached across the table and held my hand, squeezing it gently.

Look after yourself.

You too.

Look, I really am sorry, I just can't talk just now.

It's OK, just go, I'll be fine.

He stood up and walked past me, brushing against my shoulder on the way out. I stared at the empty seat in front of me.

Spaghetti vongole?
Thank you.
Black pepper? And Parmesan?
She flourished the pepper mill, spooned Parmesan over the dish, then left.

Steam rose from the spaghetti and the clam shells gleamed dully like slate roof tiles. It smelled wonderful and I was starving. I picked up my fork, twirled the pasta round and round, pressing it against the spoon, and ate.

Paul Foy   *1999*

INTERVIEW WITH A PRODDY VAMPIRE

I want you to go to Transylvania, he says, aw poncy poash like
cuz he thinks he's some soart a big shot livin oot in the sooth
side in his malky big bungalow like he does noo an callin himself Managing Director.

Is that place no full a Tims? A says back. Whit dae ye need
me tae go therr fur anywey, can ye no dae yer business bey fax?
But it's aw aboot this bloke, this stupit Count that has boaght a
hoose up the Whitecraigs an wants it decorated but he's no goat
a fax an's no oan the internet, says, Naw, he's an auld fashioned
Count an likes tae dae things face tae face an A've tae go ower
therr an draw up the plans wey him fur the interior decoration
an he's payin fur the trip an that so that's how A ends up therr.

But it's no easy tae get tae wherr his big hoose is, merr like
a big bluddy castle, so he's goney huv tae send his Landrover
doon tae pick me up at this wee soart a inn place, ye know, a
pub wey a few rooms upsterrs tae stay in if ye git too bevvied
tae be able tae make it hame, that soart a thing.

An it's aw dead nice therr in this wee part a the country, like
when A gets aff the train the station's aw wee an pokey but dead
auld an pictyerskew wey its wee flooers hangin in therr wee
basket thingies an big cherrs probably made fae oak or sumthin
an aw roon aboot is big hills an mountains, aw green an trees
at the boattom, then aw grey an craggy as ye go up a bit, an then
a big dod a snow at the top like ye always did in yer drawins a
mountains when ye wur at school, an it's no even that cauld. Aw
dead pretty an ye can just tell that Tims live here.

An this inn's full a them, aw sittin therr, lookin aboot two
centuries oot a date, wummin wey shawls roon therr heids, big
long skirts like they wurr made fey curtains, and these things
they werr roon therr bodies that make therr tits stick oot. An
the men wey the stupit hats wey the feather stickin oot the side,
big wooly sideburns coverin half therr coupons. Just like at
Parkheid. But whit's the score wey these pint glasses? A mean,
the'rr bigger than yur usual pint which is fine by me, but they've
gote these wee lids on them like the'rr teapots urr sumthin.

Anywey, A've gote a wee bit time tae kill fore A'm tae get
picked up so's, of course, A indulges in a wee bevy, soakin up
the local culture so tae speak. No bad beer either. Full bodied

stuff, if ye know whit A mean. But A'm no enjoyin mahsel cuz aw these punters urr lookin at me funny an A cin see that the'rr nominatin wan eh them tae be a spokesman fur them cuz the'rr aw soart a pushin this grey an wrinkly wee punter ower tae me an A'm thinkin, A bet they want tae know whit team A support, whether A'm a Tim ur a Proddy, that soart a thing.

So up comes this punter an he says, Where you go? Where you go? an Ah says, Who wants tae know? an he looks roon at aw the others, aw confused, an then repeats, Where you go? Where you go? so's A tells him, A'm waitin tae be picked up tae go tae the Count's place. Well, this auld punter looks like he's gonny cack his pants an then when he tells everywan they aw look like the'rr aboot tae cack therr pants anaw and the'rr pushin and pushin this auld punter right up tae me, gabberin oan like a bunch a wee lassies, and then he starts gaun oan an oan tellin me A've no tae go therr, aw in this shitty broken English, an A tells him A um goan and if he wants tae buy me a pint then that's awright, but if he disnae then wid he mind gettin himself tae buggery. Tae be honest A don't think he gote everythin that A said, but he gote the idea.

Next thing happens, A canny believe mah eyes an A'm really close tae cloutin someb'dy, A cin tell ye. First thing, they aw starts makin the sign eh the croass, like they've scored fur Celtic ur sumthin an A'm aboot tae ask ur they tryin tae take the piss ur what, an if the'rr lookin fur trouble they'll bluddy well get it, when mah jaw nearly wallops me in the bollocks. This auld wummin, this wee wifey wey a moustache hobbles forward and tries tae put a crucifix roon mah neck. Well A'm like, Ur you tryin tae be funny hen? cuz A'm tellin ye, granny ur nae granny, A'll lowp wan oan ye if ye don't git that bloody hing away fae me.

So therr's me staunin therr expectin tae get chibbed but A'm gonny take a few a them wey me when the car horn starts honkin ootside an aw these sheepshaggin local types crap therr kecks for real this time, runnin aboot mental like players in a Queen's Park v Brechin City match. Then the door comes crashin open, aw special effects like, an the'rrs naeb'dy therr cept aw this mist comin in fae the dark like the mountains huv been chain smokin an A knows that's mah cue so's A stands up aw full eh mahsel like we aw know Rangers dominate the league and we aw know who A support. An aff A steps ootside, singin, Hullo, hullo, we are the Billy boys. Ootside tae meet mah destiny.

He's quite a cool punter, smartly dressed in this soart a soaft leather long coat over Calvin Klein jeans and T-shirt. None eh yer Kappa track-suit stuff here. He's staunin next tae this big customized Landrover, like the alterations huv probably cost merr than the bluddy thing itsel, but if ye've goat money then A suppose ye can dae what ye want. An A'm thinkin eh the gaffer back hame and like, Think yu'rr poash dey ye? Then come an check this punter oot, ya manky wee nyaff that ye urr.

Anywey, he introduces himsel, tells me he's the Count an that an A says, Ferr doos, an tells him who A um an he says he knows, an A suppose we both knows but ye huv tae dae the introductions an that. So we've gote the intros over wey an we get in the caur, me sittin next tae him an as he drives aff A starts tae get the first inklin uv a suspicion cuz he disnae say anythin, jist sits therr, gies me a sideways glance an this soart a sickenin smile an A thinks, A hope this bloke isnae wan eh them hoofter types. Whitever, the bloke's a customer, an a rich wan at that so's A've goat tae try an get oan wey him – though if he tries anythin oan wey me A'm gonny bust him an therr's nae way the gaffer cin blame me fur that.

So A says tae him, standard soart a patter an that, Whit soart a school did ye go tae then?

A very private school, he says in this really toaffy voice that ye can tell is snooty even though he's gote this really thick foreign accent which is even thicker than the sheep shaggers in the pub.

Oh aye, who educated ye then? Nuns an that?

Oh no, he says and lets oot this huge laugh like A've said sumthin really funny. No nuns would come anywhere near the school I went to.

So yer no Catholic then? A asks, thinkin A might as well get tae the hert eh the matter.

Dear me no old chap, he says, but no really like that ye understaun. Ye hiv tae realise, A'm makin him sound soart a English upper-class public schoolboay, jist tae gie ye the flavour a whit he wis like. Aw superior like. Imagine that wi a bit a Boris Yeltsin an yiv goat the idea. Anywey, Dear me no, he says, My family was excommunicated many generations ago.

Well that's a relief, A'm thinkin, Ye might be a mattress muncher but at least yer no a Tim. So A tells him aboot the folk in the inn tryin tae get me tae werr a crucifix and he looks a bit uneasy fur a minute an asks if A took it but A reassure him that A'm a blue-nose and he looks relieved and tells me that the people here are a bit backward and hing oan tae these auld superstitious weys and A says that mibbe this place should twin up wey the east end a Glesga.

So wu'rr drivin up the side eh this mountin, up aw these wee windy roads wi big rocks hingin oot like the'rr gonny faw oan ye but they don't an it's aw right really cus this is a smart vehicle the auld Count hus an some mental music system an aw, pity he's listenin tae aw this classical shite. A asks him if he's gote any techno an he says naw he husnae, so A goes intae mah bag an gies him a Ibiza tape tae put oan an he's listenin away an then says somethin weird, like, Ah yes, I think I like this modern music. The beat reminds me of the blood pumping through the veins of a young virgin's arteries, an A says, Ye'll huv a joab findin any virgins oot in Ibiza, an he jist laughs an A'm thinkin he's mibbe no so bad efter aw.

Jist as we arrive at his big castle-like hoose therr's a big flash a lightenin an A think that's quite propriate cuz it makes everythin look like it's in black an white an his hoose looks like it belongs in wan eh them auld black an white fillums oan the telly like the *Addams Family* ur the *Munsters* ur sumthin. Anywey, it looks pretty cool an A canny figure why the Count wid want tae go an live in Whitecraigs, unless mibbe he's Jewish but that's awright wi me, long as we urny importin any merr Tims intae the country.

So he takes me intae the hoose an tells me that the servants ur aw oot fur the night an wu'rr aw alone in the place an A'm thinkin, Oh aye, an Ah'm gettin suspicious again but he says A've no tae worry cuz he's no gonny bite an wid A like a bite cuz before they left he hid the servant prepare a big meal fur me an he shows me intae this big room an therr's aw this poash food laid oot an he says A've tae dig in but A've please tae excuse him cuz he's no hungry an A asks him hus he any bevy an he says whitever ah want an A'm thinkin this'll dae me.

It's a big table wu'rr sittin at wi big candelabras an stuff an A'm pretty glad that he's chosen tae sit up the other end fae me cuz it his tae be said that his breath is a bit oan the bowfin side. At furst ah'm thinkin it's garlic breath, but ... well, yu'll see aboot that in a bit.

So wu'rr hivin a bit eh a natter an he's sayin how we'll go ower the plans fur his new hoose in the mornin an he's askin me how long A've been a jiner an A says, A'm no a jiner ah'm an interior decorator, an he says, Yes of course, an A'm bein polite an that but no too friendly cuz A don't want tae gie him any ideas. Thinks A, A'll talk tae him aboot the fitba, bit a lads talk, ye know. So's A asks him, When ye go aff tae live in Glesga, an he interupts wey, The suburbs, actually, old chap, an A says, Whitever. When ye move therr, whit team dae ye think ye'll support.

Well who do you support? he asks, an A says, The Gers, of course, an he says, wey a bit eh a wink A don't like, Well that shall do me then, an it's it that point that A'm cuttin intae mah stake which hus the bludd runnin oot eh it when whit dae A go and dae but cut mah bluddy finger an then it has the bludd runnin oot it anaw.

So noo he gets aw funny an his eyes go aw weird an therr's this funny noise comin fae oot his throat, like right deep doon inside, an A'm askin if he's awright when he just comes flyin ower fae the other side eh the table, grabs me – an he's a strong Count – an sticks his bluddy teeth right intae mah neck. A'm like, Get aff a me ya big jobby jabber ye, an he's goin slurp slurp an A'm feelin like a right dick wey is mingin breath aw sleazy aw ower me so's A starts thumpin im right in the temple but A cannae hurt the bugger an he lifts me right up so's mah feet urr aff the groon an kickin aboot tryin tae get his shins ur kneecaps but he jist keeps slurpin away an's no bothered.

Noo he droaps mi an A'm lyin oan the groon wi mah legs aw at funny angles an he's standin ower me wi is eyes aw red an weird lookin, an wi aw the bludd he's drunk fae me he looks like he's gote lipstick oan an A tell im he's claimed. He jist stauns therr wi is hauns oan is hips laughin an says, You should be thankful to me, for I shan't kill you. And you will show your gratitude. Soon the effects of my bite will take effect and you will join the lower ranks of the undead and shall serve me, your master.

Whit urr you oan aboot? ya big tit ye, A says tae him. He says tae me that he's a vampire an A'm gaun tae be joinin him soon an wey mah help he'll set himsel up in Glesga. Oh yes indeed, he says tae me, I really must say that you have given me a taste for blue-nosed blood.

Well, that wis enough fur me. A sees mah briefcase lyin next tae mah chair so's A grabs it an two haunded chucks it at im but he jist flaps at it wey the back eh his haun an whoosh, the whole thing jist busts open an aw mah stuff goes flyin everywhere. But, ya beauty, therr right bi mah feets lands mah souvineer fey Wembley thit A cerry wey mi whaurever A goes. It's mah bit eh the goalpost that A gote when we invaded the pitch efter beatin the English oan therr ain turf. Cuz if therr's wan thin A hate mair thin the Tims it's the Guffs. So anywey, A picks up the bit a wid an starts tae sort mahsel oot fur the attack but the Count's staunin therr wey is funny eyes an even though he's no openin is geggy A can hear im saying, You are in my power. You must do what I tell you. An right enough A feel like A'm startin tae go under his control. Then he goes, Ha ha ha. It would have been better for you if you had taken the crucifix from the peasants, an it's that thit does it fur me, A'm beelin an A gets the wid in both hauns wi the pointy bit stickin oot an A jumps up an sticks it right through that Count's hert.

Whit a scene then, A cin tell ye. He sterts thrashin aboot makin a noise like the Celtic support when Raith beat them in the cup final an aw his skin sterts shrinkin, like ye cin see noo that he hus big fangs cuz is lips urr peelin away back fae his mooth an then he jist dries up an crumples tae the flerr an aw thit's left is a pile eh dried skin an his claithes. Oh aye, an a pretty smert ring thit A pocketed fur mah troubles.

So's that's how A became a vampire, an a pain in the erse it is anaw. A mean, fur wan thing, A can noo only go tae see games at night, otherwise A'll git aw frizzled up in the sun. An A've also gote this ungoadly cravin fur bludd. A mean, if A goes tae the pub A cin still take a pint eh beer an that. The trouble noo is that it tastes like pishwater. Mind you, whit's new aboot that? But whit cin A dae? A canae exactly go intae a pub an ask fur a pint eh rhesus negative, cin A noo? They'd think A wis a poof ur sumthin. It's quite good wey the birds though. They aw tell me thit A've gote these sexy, hypnotic eyes, so's A jist sterrs it them like that Count sterred it me an Boab's yur uncle. The trouble is, A never seem tae be able tae get a shag. Like, they'll come back tae mah place awright an the'rr right intae suckin mah face, but before A know whit's happenin A'm suckin therr necks an then the'rr deid. Well they urr noo. At first A didnae know whit A wis daein an A must uv been leavin them a wee bit alive cuz noo A've gote loads eh these brides eh the undeid stoatin aboot aw wantin me tae tell them whit tae dae an askin whit huv A brote fur them tae feed oan.

So's efter A wiz turned intae a vampire an that, oot therr in Transylvania, A decided tae dae a bit eh travellin. A wiznae

too sure aboot this at first, like wis therr rules ur sumthin thit
A huv tae follow, so's A looks through the Count's library an
sure enough he's gote loads eh stuff oan the undeid an A learns
that if A wants tae travel aboot A huv tae take wey mi some
eh the turf under which A wis buried. Well that wis a bit eh a
proablem cuz A wisnae buried. Efter A killed the Count A jist
soart eh dozed aff oan the flerr an then wakened up the next
night deid an a vampire. But A wis no tae be ootdone bey the
rules eh the supernatural. Wan eh the other things A alweys
carry aboot wey me when A'm away fae hame is mah wee bit
eh the turf fae Ibrox that A keep an nurture an A found it
worked a treat. A lie in mah boax, put the turf oan mah chist
an that's me soarted.

So's Ah'll tell ye aboot mah travels in the old countries.

Here, wait a minute. Before A stert, whit time is it? Naw
sorry, yi'll hiv tae go. It's time fur the fitbaw oan the telly. Naw
don't tell me the scores, A want tae find oot fur mahsel.

A'll tell ye wan mair thing before ye go though. Yon
commentator, Gerry McNee. Is he no meant tae be a Celtic
supporter? If he is he's gonny get it in the neck wan eh these
days.

Rachel Yule   *1999*

CAVE CANEM

(passages in italics should be read in pedantic Edinburgh Scenglish)

As you can aw see –
If you're no blin –
A'm a dug:
A big, black, barkin dug,
A slinkin, snappin, snarlin dug;
An this is ma patch.
An that reid-roostit Ford pickup
Wi nae back wheels
An the door hingin aff the hinges
Is ma den.

I've seen better times.
In my – em-m – salad days
I was companion to a professor emeritus,
A scholar and a gentleman,
An Egyptologist.
When introducing me to former colleagues,
He used to say,
'I've named him Anubis. Come closer
And observe the set and shape of his ears.'
That was the sign for me tae gurr
Deep doon in ma thrapple;
Ma birse rose an ma fangs flashed.
They louped back, teeth chatterin.
'He's a one man dog,' my old boy smirked.

Oh, it was barrie – a dug's life:
Wee private jokes an every creature comfort;
Till yae day, efter a brisk constitutional
In the Queen's Park,
When he was pourin the pre-prandial sherry
He drappit doon, deid.
A was oot o ma skull, barkin mad:
A lickit his face an yowled in his lug;
But he was ayont the aid o man or beast.
So A lappit up the Tio Pepe.

I'm not proud of what happened next:
Perhaps it was the drink;
And the walk had given me an appetite;
And pangs of hunger dull the finer sensibilities;
And the name Anubis has connotations.
Onywey, efter A had reenged roon
The hale hoose an fund naethin tae eat
But a half packet o broken shortbreid,
A broke the last taboo.

A was that schizoid
A squeezed through the dug-flap
(The egress he constructed with his own hands
For my convenience when I was a little puppy,
Not quite house-trained).

Then A louped the back dyke,
An hid ma shame in Bawsinch
Amang the wee trees
In the Native Species Nursery.
I really should have had counselling.

There were beast sightings
Behind the Sheep's Heid Inn;
A Guided Walk of very mature students
Broke into a canter
Along the Innocent Railway.
Park Rangers, safe in their vans,
Screamed into their mobile phones,
'SOS! Emergency! SOS!
Send in the men from the Zoo!'

Land Rovers screamed roond the Windy Gowl;
A scarpered, an had juist about reached
The sanctuary o the Foxes' Holes
When there was a sting in ma arse –
A mere flea-bite;
Ma brain birled;
Ma legs buckled;
Samson's Ribs crumbled;
The sky blackened.

A cam roond in Seafield, c/o SSPCA.
'A'll hae that bugger,' the wee man swore.
'You quite sure? He's a killer.'
'Juist whit A'm needin.
When A got hame last nicht
Ma yaird wis hoachin wi Polis
Vandalisin upholstery, slashin tyres.'
He chucked me a bluidy great steak,
Then put the boot in ma ribs.
'He'll no bite the haun that feeds him,'
The wee nyaff gittered.
'Whit dae they cry him?'
'Anubis.' 'Whit a name for a dug!'
He luftit a bucket o cauld, dirty water.
'A hereby re-christen him, Saddam.'
Ma e'en nipped. A stank o cats.

A keep ma heid doon:
A'm a pack animal
An he's the leader o the pack – *pro tem*
(As my old mentor was wont to say).
A'm bidin ma time.
When ma day comes
A'll no bite the haun that feeds me;
A'll go for the jugular.

Stewart Conn   *2000*

KOSOVO

i   Milena

She lies at the edge of the pines,
black hair drifting over her face,
a silver earring sparkling;
alongside her mother and two brothers,
one's arm bent over his forehead
as if still cowering from the bombs.

Among the rubble, in a childlike hand,
poems to a boyfriend: *Your Milena*
still loves you. If only you knew
how much I suffer. I feel my wounds so
I don't know if I can still kiss you.
In capitals in English, again *I LOVE YOU.*

These lines and what they proclaim
all that remain as her body is loaded
on a dumper-truck and taken away.

ii   The Hunt by Night

Figures run headlong through the forest
till all are brought down. At dawn
a great exhalation shrouds the marshes,
the meadows nearby. The beasts of the field
long since gone, the fowls of the air taken flight.

iii   Ogre

We see on the screen daily
his puffy cheeks and white hair,
a man who has a price on his head.

To think he rises each morning,
does his ablutions like any other,
and passes out to the mundane air.

Disconcerting to have no sign: a malign
bubbling under the skin, or an insect
crossing the eyeball of the living man.

iv   **Hope**

Think: in the depth of the forest
a source of light – only to discover
a tiny songbird, its plumage on fire.

v   **The well**

Arc-lights blazing they detect rotting
shapes, the stench unbearable: no
grapnel could pull them out without
fear of dismemberment.
                     Suggested:
Rope a gypsy, drop him down ...

vi   **This land**

         – our birthright, who
religiously plough its hectares,
teach our children its anthem.

         – should be ours
in restitution, our forefathers
having been put to the sword.

vii   **The inheritors**

One dig unearths rows of corpses,
all male, heads aligned to the north;

Another, on the far side of the knoll,
centuries-old skeletons without skulls.

An eye for an eye, a tooth for a tooth.

viii   'What can I do for Kosovo...?'

'I cannot offer hope, far less bring
loved ones back from the dead: so what
do I do?' Then it came to her: 'I can sing.'

A fund-raising concert ended
with a radiant rendering of some
of Bach's most sublime cantatas.

ix   Exile

The school razed
to the ground, his
singing-master garrotted,

he no more dreams
of returning than
entering a roaring fire.

Far less of waiting
till his God holds
sway over theirs.

Each day he practises
to develop the muscle
cavities round his throat

x   Envoi

A new millennium
begun: lavish parties,
rapturous tolling of bells.

Here, the dominant
sound still the thud
of the gravedigger's spade.

Murdo Stal MacDonald   *2000*

EADAR ÀIRD A' MHÀSAIR IS OSTAIG

A' Chiad Latha
Craobh às deaghaidh craoibh
Air a cnòdach
Le geansaidh còinneach crotail.

An Dàrna Latha
Creamh fiathaich gham ithe
Gach madainn gu bracaist
Conas gham ithe gach tràth.

An Treas Latha
Bogha-frois' am beul a' ghlinne
Ri pògadh na mara,
'S beul fosgailt' na Linne.

An Ceathramh Latha
Cur is dlùth na coille
Air fhighe nam fhèithean
Air rathad Liosa Shlèite.

An Còigeamh Latha
Truimead na culma
Ri doth air na Garbh Chrìochan
Man leanabh air màthair.

An Siathamh Latha
Mèilich nan uan
Man seisd ri gach duan
'S a' chuthag ri togail an fhuinn.

An Seachdamh Latha
A' leigeil na mo shìneadh
Air brat-ùrlair na coille
Bròg-na-cuthaig gham thoinneamh.

An t-Ochdamh Latha
Seilleanan nam màl
'S ri leughadh na tìde,
Ri tional am bidhe gun dàil.

An Naoidheamh Latha
Neo-ar-thaing nach robh mi aoibhneach
Led sgeirean cho coibhneil
A' moladh an latha dhomh.

An Deicheamh Latha
Lòin-dhubha is smeòraich
A' cumail a' chàirdeis
Ann an càil an latha.

BETWEEN ARDVASAR AND OSTAIG

The First Day
Tree after tree
Clothed
In mossy chenille.

The Second Day
Eaten by wild garlic
For breakfast daily,
Each mealtime, I am, by gorse.

The Third Day
Rainbow touches glen
Kisses ocean
And Sound's soft lips.

The Fourth Day
Wooded warp and weft
Knitted with my veins
In the Garden of Sleat.

The Fifth Day
Heavy mists
Cling to mainland peaks
Like a child.

The Sixth Day
Lambs bleat
The chorus of the song
The cuckoo sings in tune.

The Seventh Day
Lying down to rest
On bluebell woodland carpet
Twisting, twisting.

The Eighth Day
A busy bee-body
A-weather-forecasting
A-food-collecting.

The Ninth Day
Surprised by joy
As your kind skerries
Bid me good morning.

The Tenth Day
Blackbirds and thrushes
Cèilidh-ing
In the twilight.

Brian Whittingham   *2000*

THIS SHIRT

Lies on the ironing board
like it's the creased shirt –
Undisputed Heavyweight Champion of the World.

I'm in quick –
iron setting MAX
auto 20g steam,
skooshing the spray button like a man possessed.

This shirt's surface smiles, melts onto my iron,
I survey the hot wrinkled damage

and like a *second* doing running repairs
I sandpaper the sole-plate,
wipe it clean.

Then, I'm in again –
this time, iron setting MED,
auto 15g steam.

This time I'm ladling in, I'm relentless,
the bit with the buttons
the back
the bit with the buttonholes
the sleeves
the collar ...
I stand back exhausted –

then I notice this shirt smirks triumphantly
and when I examine it closer
I see the creases are still there.
Not so pronounced this time, more subtle,
but nevertheless, still there.

It's then I realise this shirt
has once again successfully defended its crown,
and any talk of a re-match at this juncture
would be foolish on my part.

Maybe it's time I thought about hanging up my iron,
and taking stock of my future,
maybe take up a career
as a writer
where crumpled shirts are obligatory.

Margaret Beveridge   *2001*

SPEEDY DELIVERY – VERBAL ESTIMATE

Yeh, fuckin' swimming pool in here. I think your waters have
definitely broken. Let's have a look. Where's my torch?
(Muffled) You've had some cowboys in here! It wasn't a homer
last time was it? Who was it? One of those 'community' mid-
wives? (Taps speculum thoughtfully against teeth then inserts)
These piles are completely blocking your back passage, they'll
have to go. Bloody hell, these varicose veins need stripping. And
this pelvic floor is going to collapse – bladder's hanging by a
thread. How long have you had that leak? Not much room in
here... whole wall of this womb's about to come away. You
don't mind if the boys have a look. Doing an SQA module in
Obs and Gynae. Brilliant... cut the training time down from five
years to forty hours. Look at the tear in this perineum, just left
to heal naturally, for fuck's sake. You've been stitched up, love,
metaphorically speaking, that is. (muttering) Fuckin' DIY births.
Fuckin' Sheila Kitzinger has a lot to answer for. Should leave it
to the fuckin' experts. We've got the tools for it... (louder) Leave
it to the experts, love. What does your husband think?

    Need to get you down the ante-natal unit ASAP. Can't do
anything here, don't have the equipment (whistling through
teeth and shaking head). This time of the year, you're looking at
the middle of next week. Don't get excited, love. What makes
you think that was a contraction? Just leave everything to us. If
push comes to shove, best I could do is leave one of the lads
with you. Jim's still looking for a competence in live birth...
(aside) and tie off the fuckin' cord this time. Get some plastic
sheeting? Now if you go private... cash in hand, get the lads on
to it right away... Could do you a nice Caesarean section, no
extra cost. (pause) Labour's extra of course. Probably need
some cosmetic work afterwards. Pal of mine, plastic surgeon
down the private hospital, he'll see you all right. (leers meaning-
fully at the group of students) Can't just paper over the cracks
these days, can we lads? (students snicker obligingly)

    Be back in half an hour. The gear's in the ambulance, can't
shift you without it. More than my job's worth... parked three
streets away. Fuckin' traffic wardens. May as well have lunch
while we're at it. C'mon, lads. You just keep your legs open,
love, so we can let ourselves back in.

Criosaidh Dick *2001*

DILEAB

Bha i na sìneadh anns a' *bhath*, a com fon uisge agus a ceann
ri tacsa ceann a' *bhath*. 'S e *bath* mòr seann fhasanta bh' ann.
Fhuair iad e nuair a thàinig a' chiad ghrantaichean a-mach
airson taighean nan croitearan a leasachadh. Bha a mathair,
uair no dhà, a' beachdachadh air fear ùr fhaiginn ach bha h-
athair na aghaidh. 'S e duine mòr, foghainteach a bh' ann agus
bha e ag radh nach fhaigheadh e sìneadh a-mach ceart anns na
bathaichean ùra bha iad a' deanamh an diugh.

'S ann geal a bha am *bath* agus bha i na sìneadh gu socair
agus a làmhan sìos ri taobh. Bha e dìreach mar gum biodh tu
ann an ciste-laighe agus i air a lìnigeadh le sìoda geal ach gum
biodh i fuar anns a' chistidh mar a bhiodh Ruairidh Bàn, an
nàbaidh. Bha an tiodhlacadh aige ann an diugh. Bha an t-àm
aice tighinn a mach às a' bhath. Biodh iad ag èigheach rithe
greasad oirre an ceart-uair, a h-athair agus a mathair agus an
t-ogha aca, an nighean aice fhein. Bha iad uile a' dol chun an
tiodhlacaidh. 'S e deagh nàbaidh a bh' ann an Ruairidh. Bha e
mun aon aois ri pàrantan. 'S e bantrach a bh' ann. Chaochail
a bhean bho chionn dà bhliadhna. Cha robh clann idir aca.

Bha i leisg tighinn a-mach às a' *bhath*. Bha i cofhurtal na
sìneadh anns an uisge bhlàth, chùmhraidh. Bha i cofhurtal na
beatha. Bha i air a bhith a' tidseadh anns a' sgoil bheag anns a
bhaile seo, i fhein agus aon tidsear eile bho chionn corr is
fichead bliadhna. Chan iarradh i an corr. Rinn i suas a h-inntinn
nuair a bha i còig bliadhn' deug gu robh i airson a bhith na
tidsear agus gu robh i airson a bhith na tidsear anns an sgoil far
an robh i fhein nuair a bha i òg. Bha i air a bhith an-sin bhon
chrìochnaich i anns a' Cholaisde ach na sia miosan a ghabh i
dheth nuair a rugadh Donna Mairi agus 's ann glè ainneamh a
dh' fhàg i an t-eilean a' bharrachd. Seo far an robh i ag iarraidh
a bhith.

An deidh dhi bhith bliadhna a' tidseadh, bha i air a dhol
air saor-laithean dhan Spàinn comhla ri na caraidean a bh'
aice anns a' Cholaisde. Bha iad air seo a chur air dòigh anns a'
bhliadhna mu dheireadh a bha iad comhla. Bha iad gu bhith
cho math dheth, mas fhìor.

Thill i dhachaidh, donn leis a' ghrèin agus air a h-ùrachadh
leis na làithean saora agus air a h-inntinn a dhèanamh suas nach

fàgadh i an t-eilean tuilleadh. 'S e samhradh breagha blàth a bh' ann, anns a h-uile àite, a' bhliadhn' ud.

Air fear dhe na làithean breagha grianach sin, is i a' faireachdainn caran leisg, chuir i oirre tè dhe na deasachan-snàmh a bh' aice anns an Spàinn agus leine mhòr le h-athair air a h-uachdar. Thug i leatha searadair mòr agus an leabhar a bha i a' leughadh agus chaidh i sìos gu ceann shìos na croite gu oir a' chladaich. Bha bàgh beag blàth an-sin agus creagan ga fhasgadh bhon h-uile taobh. Chuir i an searadair sìos air a' ghainmheach. Bha an làn a-muigh agus bha an tràigh gheal falamh, eu-coltach ri tràighean na Spàinne, ach gu faiceadh i Ruairidh Bàn, an nàbaidh, pios uaipe, ag obair air an eathar. Biodh e a' dol a-mach leatha nuair a dh' eirigh an làn. Bha *boiler-suit* air agus leine foipe. Sin a bhiodh air an còmhnaidh. Bha faoileag no dhà a' sgiathadh os a cionn ach bha iad fhein caran leisg an diugh. Shuidh i greis a' coimhead a-mach air an traigh agus a-null chun nam beanntan fad' air falbh. 'S e deagh chomharra bha sin. Ma bha na beanntan fad' air falbh, bha an deagh shìde a' dol a mhaireachdainn. Thug i dhith a leine airson a' ghrian a' leigeil gu com agus rinn i i fhein cofhurtal air an t-searadair agus thoisich i ri leughadh an leabhair.

An ceann greis, thàinig faileas eadar i agus a' ghrian agus nuair a thog i a ceann, bha Ruairidh Bàn na sheasamh ri taobh. "Uill, uill, nach ann aig cuid a tha an saoghal dheth. Ciamar a chòrd do chuairt riut?"

Shuidh e air a' ghainmheach faisg oirre agus dh' innis i dha gun do chòrd a turas rithe uamhasach math ach gu robh i toilichte a bhith dhachaidh.

"'S e fiòr *home bird* a th'annad", thuirt e.

Bha iad a' bruidhinn a-null 's a-nall greis agus iad a' coimhead air a cheile.

"B' fheairrd thu do thuras. Tha a' ghrian air laighe gu mòr ort. Tha e tighinn math dhuit."

Bha e air tighinn na b' fhaisg' oirre.

Bha i na leth shìneadh air a h- uileann a' coimhead suas na aodann. Shìn i i fhein a-mach mar chat ga bhlianadh fhein as a' ghrèin. Bha e cho nàdurra mar a thog i suas a làmhan agus chuir i mu amhaich iad agus tharraing i e a-nuas gus a pògadh. Dh' fhàs na pògan na bu mhiannaiche. Thog e a làmh agus thug e na strapaichean bhar a gualainn agus thoisich e ri pògadh a ciòchan.

Thog e a cheann agus choimhead e oirre.

"A bheil thu cinnteach gur e seo a tha thu ag iarraidh?"

"Tha, tha mi glè chinnteach."

Chaidh mìos seachad agus da mhiòs agus bha i cinnteach gu robh i trom. Dh' fheumadh i dhol chun an dotair ach cha robh feum aic' air dearbhadh. Bha i air a bhith cinnteach bhon chiad latha gum biodh i trom.

Nuair a dh' innis i dha h-athair is dha mathair bha an cridheachan briste. Cha robh iad airson a creidsinn. Chan innseadh i dhaibh cò leis a bha e. Am b' aithne dhaibh e? An robh seo air tachairt nuair a bha i air falbh air na saor-laithean? An e Spàinnteach a bh' ann? Bha iad a' fàs fiathaich. An e nach robh fhios aice? Mo nàire! Bhiodh gu leòr aig muinntir a' bhaile ri radha.

Thuirt i riutha, nan robh iad airson, gun gluaiseadh i a-mach às an taigh. Gheibheadh i taigh-comhairle. Agus phàigheadh i cuid-eigin airson coimhead as dèidh an leanaibh fhads a bha i ag obair.

Tha fios nach robh dùil aice tilleadh a dh' obair. A h-aghaidh a chur air clann-sgoile. An leigeadh iad leatha tilleadh dhan sgoil?

Ach mu dheireadh striochd iad agus cha robh chrith aice a bhith a' smaoineachadh air a dachaidh fhàgail. Cò b' fheàrr a choimheadadh as a dèidh na a h-athair agus a mathair fhein? Agus nuair a thigeadh an leanabh, nach eil fhios gur ann aig a sheanair agus a sheanmhair a bha còir coimhead as a dheidh cuideachd. Cha robh iad gus a bhith air an nàrachadh buileach glan.

Ma bha muinntir a' bhaile ri foghail, cha tuirt duine guth riuth-san. Biodh i a' cluinntin a mathair a' rànaich uaireanan air feadh na h-oidhche agus a h-athair ga cofhurtachadh, ach beag air bheag, bh' fhàs cùisean na b' fheàrr agus nuair a rugadh an leanabh bha iad cho toilichte agus cho measail oirre agus ged nach biodh na mìosan a chaidh seachad air tachairt riamh.

Dè an t-ainm a bha i a' dol a thoirt oirre? "Bha mi a' smaoineachadh, nam biodh sibh fhein deònach, gun toirinn na h-ainmean agaibh fhein oirre. Donna Mairi – Domhnall agus Mairi." Choimhead a h-athair agus a mathair air a chèile. Bha deòir na suilean. "Chòrdadh sin rinn math dha rireabh," thuirt a h-athair.

Aon latha is a h-athair agus a mathair air falbh fon taigh agus i fhein trang ag obair air leabhraichean sgoile, thog i a h-aire far an tè bhig. Aon mhionaid bha i a' cluich mun doras agus an ath mhionaid cha robh sgial oirre. Chlisg i. Chaill a casan an lùths.

Ach direach leis a-sin, nochd an nàbaidh, Ruairidh Bàn, timcheall ceann na bathchadh agus an tè bheag aige air a ghualainn.

"Thachair i rium," ars esan, "a' dèanamh air a chladach."

"O, taing dhan Aigh."

Chuir e sìos Donna Mairi agus chaidh i na ruith a-staigh dhan taigh.

"An ann leamsa tha i? Mas ann, bhithinn deònach gabhail rithe."

'S e duine onarach a bh' ann, smaoinich i.

"Chan ann, 's ann leamsa tha i." Bha i a' smaoineachadh gun tàinig faochadh air aghaidh.

Bha Donna Mairi a-nis fichead bliadhna. Bha an ceathrar ac' air a bhith glè chofhurtal comhla. 'S e mamaidh a bh' aig Donna Mairi oirre-se agus seanair agus seanmhair air a pàrantan. Bha iad an toiseach a' smaointeachadh gum bu chòir do Donna Mairi a bhith a' gabhail mamaidh agus dadaidh orra-san ach thuirt ise gur ann leath-se bha i agus gur e mamaidh a bhiodh aic' oirre.

Ged a dh' fhoighneachd Donna Mairi aig amanan nuair a bha i ag èirigh suas cò b' athair dhi, thuig i mu dheireadh nach robhar a' dol a dh' innse dhi agus stad i. Mas do dh' fhalbh i dhan Oilthigh dh' fhoighneachd i aon uair eile agus cha do dh' fhoighneachd tuilleadh.

Thàinig crith oirre. Bha an t-uisg' air fàs fuar. Seo mar a bhiodh e ann an ciste-laighe. Thàinig i a-mach às a' *bhath* agus thiormaich i i fhein. Chuir i oirre *dressing-gown* agus chaidh i tron chidsin airson a dhol suas an staidhre a chur iompa. Bha h-athair agus a mathair deiseil mar tha. Bha iad na suidhe aig a' bhord ag òl cupa tì. An robh i ag iarraidh cupa? Bha i an àm greasad oirre. Cha robh. Rachadh i a chur iompa.

Bha Donna Mairi a-muigh anns a' ghàrradh. Bha ise deiseil cuideachd. Bha gàrradh breagha aca. Bha a h-athair deidheil air flùraichean. Choimhead i a-mach air an uinneig. Bha Donna Mairi na seasamh agus ròs dearg aice na laimh.

Bha sluagh mòr anns an eaglais. Bha daoine measail air Ruairidh Bàn. Agus bha seasamh aige anns an àite. Ach cha robh càirdean dlùth idir aige. Bha na càirdean a bh' aige caran fad' às. Cha robh duin' ann, a chanadh tu, bhiodh ga chaoidh.

Air an rathad dhachaidh anns a' chàr bha Donna Mairi ag

radh gur e tiodhlacadh uamhasach duilich a bh' ann. "Uill,"
ars' a seanmhair, "tha a h-uile tiodhlacadh duilich. Tha daoine
a' caoidh."

"Sin, ged tha, a tha deanamh an tiodhlacadh seo cho
duilich," thuirt Donna Mairi. "Bha Ruairidh Bàn cho laghach
agus chan eil duine ga chaoidh." Bha iad uile samhach airson
greis. "Thug e litir dhomhsa mas do dh' fhalbh mi dhan
Oilthigh. Dh' iarr e orm a cur air falach agus gun innse do
dhuine. Agus thug e orm gealltainn nach leughainn i gus am
biodh e marbh agus air a thiodhlacadh."

"Tha sin annasach," thiurt a seanmhair. "Saoil dè th'as an
litir?" An do dh fhosgail thu i?

"Cha do dh' fhosgail. Gheall mi dha nach fosglainn i gus am
biodh an tiodhlacadh aige seachad. Thug e orm mionnachadh."

Cha tuirt i facal agus cha chanadh.

Nuair a chaidh iad dhachaidh, chaidh Donna Mairi suas
an staidhre a dh' iarraidh na litreach.

Bha e air a' chroit agus na beathaichean agus an taigh –
taigh breagha cloiche – agus an eathar agus na bha aige anns
a' bhanca fhagail aice. Cha robh an corr anns an litir. Cha tuirt
duine facal.

"'S e m' athair a bh' ann, nach e? Bha còir aig cuid-eigin a
bhith air innse dhomh."

James Robertson   *2001*

RENÉ MAGRITTE IN EMBRO

As I wis gaun by Moray Place
I met a gent in bowler-hat
An overcoat, an mair nor that
He had an aipple in his face.

I trauchelt ower tae Royal Circus:
Leaves were birds, the birds were stane.
I heard a moothless wife mak mane:
'Wurds are symbols sent tae irk us.'

A German sausage in a helmet
Had aw the New Town leddies keekin,
For he wis baith a coorse an sleek yin,
An gart them twitch frae hem tae pelmet.

A muckle boolder in the lift
Wis floatin ower the gurlie sea.
Coffins on a balcony
Were no impressed. They didna shift.

The toun lay in the mirk black nicht
As I gaed on tae Charlotte Square;
A torso, tuba an a chair
Hung in the air sae blue an bricht.

An artist lad on Princes Street
Wis drawin croods wi chalk an wiper.
Says he, 'Ceci n'est pas un piper',
An signed himsel 'Rennie Mackay'.

I daunert syne by Randolph Crescent,
Whaur clootie-heidit luvers bide.
The trees were fittit oot inside,
An aw the hooses arborescent.

An at a hoose by Telford's brig
It seemed the neibourheid wis tense:
An aipple'd taen up residence,
An it wis green an affie big.

On Belford Road I had a seat,
Tho it wis in a bonnie bleeze.
The blocks were blawin in the breeze.
I left ma shuin inside ma feet.

A broken landscape on the flair,
A path across the canvas gress.
I stude forenent the windae gless,
An saw a view that wisna there.

I passed the Dean an gaed in ben,
For it wis rainin businessmen.

Ian Stephen

FISH-SOUP – A RECIPE

You take a large wooden fishing boat which has been too good at catching small fish and so starving other fish and seabirds. You don't worry. *Fear Not* because this scale of hunting has within it the seeds of its own destruction. You wait until it's been decommissioned from fishing and is being broken up with chainsaws and diggers. You reserve large pieces of oak – the breasthook, ribs... and set aside. You maintain a small boat, using that oak from the larger one where necessary, to replace parts. Conserve the sawdust. Set aside. You source ballast stones, from the Baltic coasts, in the same way that Baltic traders came in ballast to Stornoway. Dumped their stones here to take instead the weight of whitewood barrels packed with herring. Left behind a small islet they call Little Russia. And some folding-money. The cash is gone but some of the smooth stones are left.

You've been to the Baltic. German side. Former-East. East is a relative measure. You've taken some more smooth stones back home, a continuity of trade. This ballast lends stability to that same smaller, older boat. In winter you line up the land-marks you were shown as a spotty kid. They still work. You find a reef and lower lures made from old chrome: car-door handles; offcuts from pramwheels. Mackerel or squid bait sends out a slick from a trailing hook. You fish the drift, over and over the reef and wait out the cold on the hands. Wish you'd brought more socks, thicker clothes. But the tugging comes and then the verdigris shape of the cod. Its changing colours on the bleached stones. Then the shoal of green and white coalfish grows beside the cod, on the ballast.

You gut the fillet in one, down the backbones. The white of the cod, grey of the coalfish is placed in brine. Oak dust from the decommissioned *Fear Not* is set on a steel tray over a meths burner. It's from a Danish version of a fondue-set. This *Fear Not* was built in Denmark. The oak sends up pungent smoke. Bricks collected from the demolitions of Rugen (the same source as the ballast stones) are built, dry, around the burner. The stiff fillets are placed on a grid spaced from the burner but in the smoke. The whole assembly is closed with a stainless-steel hood found on yet another shore. The tideline of Tolsta, Lewis, the village which claimed the name of *Fear Not* for its boats. First a clinker wooden beach-boat, powered by a lug sail and a second cousin of your own small surviving old boat. Then the favoured Tolsta name was transferred to progressively larger vessels. Until you had the powerful, Danish-built hull. A fine vessel in herself but misused by chasing the sandeels and pout which should have fed the cod, the haddock, the puffins and gannets and migrating sea-trout. Which made good money from fishmeal suppliers and mink-food wholesalers.

Now the remains of the massive hull are smoking the white-fish which still shoal on the reefs they can't yet drag. Sufficient oak dust for sufficient smoke to curl, hidden, into the fillets. They cool. They are set aside along with the stock made from boiling the cod's head and the backbones of the coalfish.

This is shopping. Some people do this on Saturday afternoons instead of going fishing. You source red onions and white ones, fresh dill and parsley. Scottish butter. Should it have been Lurpak? Equal quantities of each? Desiree potatoes.

You peel rose skins to show waxy yellow and the faintest tinge of green. Onions move towards the transparent, in the butter but maintain the integrity of pink and white. Wax cubes join them and the first of the smokies. You mustn't be in a hurry to add the stock. A little of the greenery now to infuse flavour but most of it reserved to yield fresh green speckled with pepper over the remaining flaked fillets. Not before you've balanced the dish with full-cream milk and some extra cream.

The soda-bread in rounds, to be broken to steam when the close of the song signals. Taste for seasoning. *Fear Not*, it'll be OK.

Jim Carruth   2002

THE BALEMARTIN BARD

He could be gone for days

moving between the ceilidh houses
of neighbouring townships.

Even in his absence
they came to the croft,

the daughters and sons of cottars,
appearing in ones and twos

from the long grass of the machair,
ragged and hungry for new words.

Leaving the chores
his sister welcomed them all.

Her rough hands would point
below the sagging lintel

to the driftwood door
where he had carelessly scribbled

his most recent bardachd.
She would read it to them

as slowly as the tides turn
letting the music of each line

fill their ears.
In the singing voices

that departed across the fields
she would listen

for the echo of her brother.

Gerry Loose   *2002*

From: SYNCHRONICITIES

three hundred years ago the poet Basho was walking steadily
north from the capital   pausing at Sendai he met the painter
Kaemon   when they parted the artist gave the poet a pair
of sandals   a useful gift for a walker   laces dyed that exact
& unfathomed blue of an iris
about which Basho makes a poem

reading the poem   I walk from my house under blown cloud
to the Botanic Gardens   passing where Muslim sells flowers
in a tub he has iris for sale the precise colour of Basho's laces
I greet him & for less than the price of a loaf buy ten
violet flags   equal parts bruised cloud & sunshaft

we nearly did a deal on the mare & her foal at foot
after haymaking   rain starting   Tim O'Sullivan
drove off on his cabless tractor
of course he took my old duffel coat for its hood
in the tractor shed a wren built her nest in the coat pocket
& the following summer ripening
Tim rode across the bog to return it
nest eggs chicks how could he disturb her

thirty years & five floors up   on the balcony in the pot with
a clump of fern   a city pigeon has laid two
alabaster eggs   on a small clutching   of red
& yellow cut electrical wires
& I cannot go out there   even for soft spring rain

I was on fire & her cool hands quenched me
I was on fire & her hands fanned the flames

she stitched the straps of a poem to shorten it
as I put words to my silent dress

the Cubans sing on tape
what it's really like to be old

gently like mother flesh
touched & left in vacancy

bam ban and gone   into the mirror
she smoothes down her silk dress

belly, backs of thighs & waist
bam ban   a time

how today
a small redemption is given me
as the barman takes back
my untasted pint of Guinness
poured by the new barwoman
& unasked tops it
to the measure   black
after my daughter's unstated
grief had wet my
foolish eyes
& she spoke of dreams
& my cigarette burns
unheeded in the ashtray
as I write
in this bar
what is given

how we still wake in the morning
what it is you're afraid of
death perhaps, did not come &
how many comets & lunar eclipses
we miss.   my daughter sleeps now & I
smoke my last half cigarette & put
the moon back again   some ducks fly past
you there   me here   Glasgow

David S. Mackenzie   2002

GILFEDDER

Gilfedder said: *It's not easy with a sore stomach.*
It's what? I said.
Difficult, he said, *difficult to lift a crate when you've a sore stomach.* And then he punched me hard in the solar plexus.

I doubled over and fell to my knees. My eyes watered and I gasped like a wheezy old bellows.

Gilfedder leaned over and spoke to me quietly, in my ear: *I run this place, right? And I don't like fancy cunts like you. Right? This is a man's job, this, so you've no fuckin' chance.* Then he straightened up and walked away.

I managed to pull myself up and sit on a chair. I leaned forward and spread myself across the formica-topped table, one of three in the empty staff room. I lay like this for a full minute, trying to regulate my breathing. Then I sat up. My stomach hurt like hell. I wasn't sure I could even stand, far less lift a crate of fish. But I did stand up. I picked up my red rubber gloves from the table and stumbled towards the door. I steadied myself against the wall as I made my way slowly along the corridor that led to the loading bay.

I held myself pretty much erect as I walked across the floor to join the other men who were already starting to unload the lorry that had drawn up alongside the bay. Each wooden crate of fish was grabbed by two men, one each end, and swung down from the lorry onto a pallet made of thick slats of pine. A couple of men stood on the lorry itself and shifted the crates into position for the unloaders. The whole place was cold and everything smelled of fish.

Morgan, the night shift leader, said: *Gilfedder, you work with the new man.*

I'm no workin' with that, Gilfedder said, without looking round. He had decided to lift the crates by himself and he did so with ease, taking hold of them as if they were empty and flinging them down on the pallets. Lumps of ice from the crates scattered across the floor of the loading bay. *Mind and no spill any,* Morgan said but Gilfedder gave no indication he'd heard. To me Morgan said: *Up on the lorry, then, and give Bob and the Mule a hand.* I did as I was bidden.

Of course Gilfedder was right: it was very difficult for me

to lift the crates when my stomach ached so much. I started slowly, got slower still but managed to recover later on.

The bed of the lorry and the stone floor of the loading bay were the same height so when only a couple of layers of crates remained on the lorry we were no longer dropping crates down onto the pallets, we were building the pallets up. Most of the men were now on the lorry. I found myself next to Gilfedder. *How's the new cunt?* he said to me. *Oh fine,* I replied. I managed to pick up a crate by myself and I flung it up onto the rising levels of the nearest pallet. A herring slipped out and landed at my feet. *Mind and no spill any, new cunt,* Gilfedder said. I picked up the herring and flung it into the nearest crate.

When the lorry was unloaded we trooped through to the freezing room. It was as if we were still outside. The freezing room was a huge hall with a high ceiling and it was filled with cold air, the stink of fish and the loud purring of the motors that powered the freezing vats. Bob and the Mule had left their early job on the lorry and had moved the fully laden pallets through from the loading bay using forklift trucks. The pallets were now lined up next to the freezing vats.

Morgan said: *Right, let's fill the bastards.*

Again, we worked in pairs, emptying the crates into the vats. We had to spread the fish carefully so that they slipped down between the vertical metal plates inside the vats. These plates were about four inches apart. When each vat was full of fish they were all sprayed with water until the vats held only vertical slices four inches thick and made out of water and tightly packed fish. Then the freezing began. Within half an hour the fish were frozen into slabs. The slabs were then pushed up from below until they stuck up above the vats and could be snapped off, stacked on pallets and driven round to the cold room for storage.

It took fifteen minutes or so to fill all seven vats with fish and thirty minutes for the vats to freeze completely. This meant that when we had finished filling the vats we had about fifteen minutes to wait until the first vat was ready for emptying. Assuming there wasn't another lorry to be unloaded, we could have a break. We went back through to the staff room.

This was a small room completely without adornment. The yellow walls were bare. The pale blue tops of the formica tables were stained with odd spots and rings of tea and coffee and spilled cigarette ash. There were fifteen chairs made of tubular metal and with plastic seats and backs. The two ceiling lights were extremely bright as if to convince us we were working during the day, not at night. The place stank of cigarettes and fish. The men took off their dark red rubber aprons and flung them on the backs of the chairs. They took out their piece boxes from their haversacks and ate their sandwiches. They drank from thermos flasks. When they'd eaten and drunk they got out their roll-up tins and made cigarettes whose smoke rose, gathered and settled in a layer just above head height. There was little conversation apart from speculation as to the arrival time of the next lorry. Then Gilfedder said, loudly, so that no one could miss him: *How's the new boy doin'?*

Oh, just fine, I said. *Just fine.*

Stomach OK?

Never better.

Then the Mule, who was a man in his early sixties, said to Gilfedder: *Leave the lad alone, Donnie. He'll be just grand if you let him be.*

Keep out o' this, Mule, Gilfedder said. *If he's a lad then he shouldna be here. This is man's work.*

I looked at Gilfedder properly for the first time. I guessed he was about thirty years old. He was quite a big man – about six feet tall – and very broad. Although the same height as me he must have been a couple of stones heavier and none of this was fat. He was physically fit and robust but his face betrayed him, displaying to those who could read it, the mixture of strengths and weaknesses afforded by his physique. For he had a look that bordered on desperation, as if it was necessary for him to assert his physical superiority moment by moment. And his expression made me feel that if this confirmation were denied him then something inside him might fragment with consequences that were unpredictable but almost certainly bad.

Man's work, he said again, looking across at me. *This is fucking man's work.*

I knew I had to say something but invention left me. I was glad that Morgan came in to announce the arrival of the next lorry. Piece boxes were closed, thermoses capped and aprons were tied on again. We went back out to the loading bay.

The night shift finished at eight o'clock, just as it was beginning to get light. Someone had let down the tyres on my bike. Gilfedder, I supposed. At least he hadn't slashed them. I pumped them up and then cycled home.

• • •

I didn't sleep much that day for thinking about the job and Gilfedder and wondering if I could survive either. I decided to build myself a breastplate made of tin with long thin sharp nails protruding on one side. I would goad Gilfedder into hitting me in the stomach again and watch him scream in agony as he smashed his knuckles into the needle-like points of the nails.

Because I wanted to hurt Gilfedder; I wanted to hurt him very much indeed. It didn't matter to me if he was off work for weeks and then lost his job. I couldn't understand how someone so evil could exist at all. He was a bad man and I wanted to hurt him badly. With this vengeance in mind I managed to fall asleep for a couple of hours. When I woke up I felt more tired than before and my stomach hurt where Gilfedder had punched me. And I was depressed. My breastplate of nails idea was ridiculous. Any type of retaliation was silly. Escalation of conflict. I could see a future of knuckle-dusters and baseball bats, maybe even knives. When it came to violence Gilfedder was an expert; I was a rank amateur. I decided that the only way I might overcome him would be to take everything he dished out and respond only with silence. After a while he would get bored with the whole enterprise. It wasn't much of a strategy but it was the only one I had.

At the beginning of the next shift he slapped me on the back. Hard. *Come back for more, eh, new cunt? I thought you'd have more sense, educated bastard like you.* I turned and looked at him but said nothing. *No speakin', eh?* He smiled at me. I walked out into the loading bay. We started on the first lorry. As usual Gilfedder worked alone. I started off working with the Mule. At one point Morgan left the loading bay and went into the freezing room to check the vats. I heard Gilfedder shout: *Hey, new cunt, catch!* I turned to see something flying towards me. Instinctively I put my hands up to my face and this thing thudded into them. It was a dogfish. They often turned up among the herring. They were strange creatures, long and thin like stretched out sharks. When you dipped your hands into the herring boxes you had to be careful because dogfish have a long sharp spike that sticks up at the trailing edge of the dorsal fin. Sometimes you knew you'd found a dogfish only when this spur hit you, went through your glove and into your hand. The cut could be deep and painful. As it was on this occasion because it was the back of the fish that hit my palms and the spur entered my hand at the base of my right thumb. I doubled up in pain. There was a lot of laughter, all from the one man.

He's a bugger, that man, the Mule said to me quietly as he inspected my hand which was oozing blood. *Just go through to the office and ask for the first aid box.*

I did as he suggested. Gilfedder watched me go and laughed some more. When I got back, having dabbed the wound with antiseptic and stuck a plaster on it, I said nothing to anyone. I got a fresh pair of gloves from the store and carried on working. *Well!* Gilfedder said loudly, as usual. *Second shift and already got through your first pair of gloves. What a hard worker we've got here, eh?* I ignored him.

In the morning, at the end of the shift, my tyres were flat again. This time they had been slashed. I wheeled the bike home. I slept for four hours and dreamed of herring. I was in the sea with them, shoals of them swimming round me, and I was trying to catch them. I was wearing a pair of enormous red gloves and perhaps my hands, too, were enormous inside them. I reached out and tried to snatch the fish as they swam past. I didn't catch any. I got up and wheeled the bike into town. I got new tyres and inner tubes and cycled back. At seven thirty I cycled to work for the start of my third shift.

Hey, how's the bike? Gilfedder asked me when I walked into the staff room. I ignored him but I sat down at the same table he was sitting at. There was no one else at that table. *I said how's the bike?* Gilfedder repeated, but I said nothing. I took my piece box from my bag and put it on the table. *I fuckin' asked you a question,* Gilfedder said and his tone had moved from derision to menace. I continued to ignore him. A hand reached over and swiped the piece box from in front of me. Luckily the lid was still on. It landed on the floor by the door, right at the feet of Morgan who was just stepping in. Bewildered, Morgan picked it up. *Whose is this?* he asked. I stood up. *Mine,* I said and I took it from him. *Lorry's in,* Morgan said and we all went out to the loading bay.

Gilfedder's big joke on that third night was to fill my piece box with herring guts. He laughed when I opened the box and found my sandwiches inedible but I said nothing. I knew I'd be very hungry but I still said nothing. I drank my tea in silence. I carefully sniffed the tea first, believing that he might have pissed in it but he hadn't. Maybe he was saving that for the next night. *Eat your sandwiches, why don't you, eh?* he said. I continued to ignore him. *Hey, new cunt, I'm talkin' to you. I'm fuckin' talkin' to you.* He leaned over the table.

I knew the next thing would be a hand swiping at my mug, and I was right. I just moved the mug back out of Gilfedder's reach and he missed. Not only that but in trying to deliver the blow he'd overstretched himself and he lost his footing on the slippery tiles of the floor. He tumbled over, catching his side on the corner of the table and he landed on the floor in a heap. Everyone in the staff room, except me, burst out laughing. I carried on drinking my tea.

As he got up from the floor Gilfedder winced very slightly, just enough to show that he had done himself some damage as he fell.

But when he managed to stand up, leaning on the table for support, he was more enraged than before. *Which o' you cunts was laughin' at me!* he screamed at us. I wanted to say: *Every-one,* but I didn't. The Mule said it for me.

We all laughed, ye daft gowk, he said. *You fair excelled yourself there.*

I'll brain any man that laughs at me, Gilfedder shouted.

Well, you'll just have to wipe out the entire gang o' us then, the Mule went on in his usual quietly amused fashion. *Which is fine if you fancy unloading all those lorries just by yourself.*

Gilfedder stood there for a few moments without saying anything. He was full of anger which hadn't yet found a way out. He turned to look at me. I knew he was looking at me because he seemed to be turned in my direction but I was not looking at him. This was part of my plan. I would never talk to him and never look at him. But I knew he was looking at me. I was nearest, just across the table. He could easily hit me now; there was nothing to stop him. I expected him to hit me. I might try to move away but I would not retaliate. I would not retali-ate because that's what he wanted me to do. I sipped my tea and waited for the blow.

But he didn't hit me. He just pointed at me. He pointed at me and said: *I'll fix you, you cunt. I'll fuckin' fix you.*

Now he was a little boy in the playground, reduced to making threats. I decided I was winning.

During the course of the next hour it became clear that Gilfedder
was struggling. He continued to work alone when unloading the
lorries but the fluency with which he plucked the crates from the
stack and flung them down on the pallets was not there any
more. He began to keep his right arm tucked close in to his body
so that he looked lopsided and awkward. The other men
noticed this too. I could see nods in Gilfedder's direction and I
heard them muttering that it served the bastard right.

By six in the morning when the fifth lorry of the night
arrived Gilfedder was still working alone but he was moving
slowly. He was clearly in pain. I tried to feel sorry for him but I
couldn't. Morgan came over to me and said: *Give Gilfedder a
hand, will you, Tom.* The nearest men paused in their work and
looked over at the two of us. Gilfedder was standing to one side,
breathing heavily. I wasn't sure if he'd heard Morgan's request
but I made sure he heard my reply. I said: *I'm not working with
that.* I rejoined the Mule and we worked together till the end of
the shift. No one spoke to Gilfedder. Everyone left him to work
at his own pace which became slower and slower. During the
breaks he sat at the same table as me in the staff room but he
said nothing to anyone. At seven o'clock Morgan said to him:
Why don't you go home if you're in pain? And someone added,
quietly: *Aye, and fuckin' stay there for the rest of your life.* But
Gilfedder shook his head. He was determined to make it to the
end of the shift. And he did.

But he didn't turn up for work the following evening.
Cracked rib, Morgan reported when someone finally got round
to asking, during the first break. *He'll be off for a while, too.
Great shame, he's a good man.*

Define 'good', the Mule asked but Morgan didn't reply.

Someone else said: *How long's a while?*

Morgan thought for a moment. *Signed off for a month, I
think,* he said.

Could you not make it two?

Morgan looked at the man who had spoken. The rest of the
men laughed. *So what's wrong with Gilfedder, then?* Morgan
asked.

What's right wi' him, more like, the Mule said.

Well, he works hard, Morgan replied.

Does he work any harder than any of the rest of us? the
Mule countered.

Morgan looked round the assembled men. After a silence

that lasted too long, he said: *Well, no, I wouldn't say that, no.*
A few moments later he left the room.

Then the Mule said: *Daft or what? If Gilfedder's the biggest bastard in the world, then Morgan's the daftest. Canna see what's starin' him in the face.*

But when you think of him workin' wi' a cracked rib, Morrison said.

What?

Gilfedder, workin' wi' a cracked rib.

So?

Well, I'm just sayin'...pride, I don't know...

Well, the Mule went on, *it's not pride if you ask me, it's his damn hard head. You're not takin' his side now, are you?*

No, no. I'm just sayin'...

Just sayin' what?

Well, that you've got to hand it to him, that's all...

Hand it to him? By God I'd fuckin' hand it to him. You're beginning to sound like Morgan.

And at that point Morgan returned and announced that the fish were now frozen and it was time to get them out and stacked.

While Gilfedder was away, things were so much easier. I even began to enjoy the work. The fact that Gilfedder would inevitably return was a threat, of course, but not for the first week, at least. I got to know some of the men and I began to learn from them about how to work more efficiently – how not to tire myself out in the first couple of hours of my shift. They taught me by example a number of things which were apparently very simple but also very useful. I learned the correct way to lift a box of fish so that I didn't expend too much energy. If I needed to lift it two feet then that was precisely how far I should lift it. Not three feet or even two feet and an inch. Just two feet. *Push and slide as much as possible,* the Mule told me. *And when you're lifting, use your legs as much as possible. Don't lean over. Bend your legs then straighten. They're stronger than your arms, after all. And don't charge at the work. It's a long race this, not a sprint.*

So what about Gilfedder? I asked him.

What about him?

All this business about not charging at the work. That's exactly what he does.

The Mule shook his head. *You're right,* he said. *You're right.*

*Don't know where he gets the energy from. So much fuckin'
energy he canna keep it in.*

Mostly it was my doing but often the talk came back to
Gilfedder. I learned a lot about him, or rather, I learned a lot
about what people believed of him. And there were many
contradictions. Morrison swore on his life that Gilfedder's
father had been a miner and had died in a pit accident when
Gilfedder was eight years old. But Bob had met a cousin of
Gilfedder's when he was on a construction job in Aberdeen and
he'd said that Gilfedder's father had been in the Army and had
died in a car accident up in Caithness, somewhere near Halkirk.

One of the men had been at school with Gilfedder but even
he seemed unsure about the facts. Gilfedder had been suspended
from school several times but he couldn't bring to mind the
details of any of Gilfedder's offences. Certainly Gilfedder had
played football for the school and he'd even had a trial for a
team in one of the Scottish divisions – Motherwell, he thought.
Morrison said no, it was definitely Celtic but everyone laughed
at this. Anyway, all were agreed that whichever team was
involved nothing had come of it. Like most of his classmates at
school, Gilfedder had wound up in a succession of labouring
jobs. This was his second stint at the fish factory. He'd spent a
year here about three years ago but left for a better job on a
construction site on the West Coast. When that job ended he'd
come back and been rehired here straight away.

They like him because he works hard, the Mule said, shaking his head.

Well, he does work hard, doesn't he? Morrison offered.

Would you employ him then?

Well, no, I wouldn't.

And why not?

Well, he's...

He's no right in the head, the Mule said. *Clean daft and
dangerous with it. Should be in Nain House, if you ask me.*

He's been there, Morrison said.

What?

He's been there. Twice that I know of.

Now he tells us.

What happened? I asked.

Oh, it was a while ago now, Morrison said.

A while ago? the Mule asked.

Years ago. Ancient history.

So?
So what?
So why did they put him in there? the Mule asked.
Yes. What happened? I repeated.

It was clear that Morrison now regretted having mentioned the issue. *I'm no sayin' nothing more,* he said, but then added: *He wasnae long out of school. A long time ago. All forgotten now.*

You haven't forgotten it, the Mule said. *And I'm damn sure Gilfedder hasn't forgotten it.*

It's nothing, Morrison said. *It's... I shouldna have mentioned it at all.*

Damn right you shouldna have mentioned it, Bob said. *I imagine Gilfedder'll no be too pleased either.*

Don't none of you fuckin' mention this to him, Morrison said. *Not a fuckin' word.* For a moment he looked genuinely scared.

Just tell us why, the Mule said. *Just tell us why he was in there. We'll no say a word. None of us.* There were murmurs of approval from round the room. *Come on.*

Morrison looked at us. He looked over at the men sitting at the other tables. *Not a fuckin' word, right?*

We all agreed to this. *Not a word. Don't worry. Nothing. Not a word.*

Morrison looked down at the open sandwich box in front of him. *Depression,* he said. *Tried to kill himself.*

Someone said: *No!* in a voice of quiet surprise. Then there was a short silence until the Mule said: *Twice?*

Morrison nodded. *Twice.*

Someone said: *Poor bastard. Would you believe it? Poor bastard.*

Someone else said: *Poor bastard my arse. Two chances to be rid of the bugger and neither of them came off.*

Gilfedder may have been signed off for a month as Morgan had suggested but he was back within two weeks. He was first in the staff room at the beginning of the shift, sitting at his usual table. He winked at me when I came in and he must have noticed the surprise on my face, though I said nothing. I sat down and emptied my haversack as usual and I didn't say anything. Nor did he say anything to me but I knew he was looking at me. As the men trooped in there were a lot of surprised faces. *So soon?*

someone said, and someone else said: *Aye, Donnie, how's the ribs, eh?* But he said nothing in reply, nothing at all. He spoke to no one and this was new and it made me afraid.

When we got to the loading bay to tackle the first lorry of the night, Gilfedder tore into the stacks of boxes as if his two week absence had been for special training rather than convalescence. His work rate through the first two hours of the shift was so high that even Morgan found it hard to believe. *Will you look at that,* he said to no one in particular. *God almighty, what's that man on?* The Mule said: *Diesel, most like. Gives you a fair boost, eh?*

Gillfedder's huge energy and drive depressed me because his injury had obviously not slowed him down at all, nor subdued him in the slightest. And his silence was unnerving. It didn't strike me until much later that he might be using the same tactics as me. But whereas my silence was that of feigned indifference, his was all about the creation of menace.

At the end of the first break, during which he didn't say a word to anyone, he was one of the last to leave the staff room. I stayed until he'd been gone perhaps half a minute before I too set off back to the loading bay. But he was waiting for me in the corridor. And he spoke for the first time that night.

Well, well, he said to me. *You're still here, eh?*

I said nothing and made to pass him. He grabbed me by the lapels. *Just a wee word, that's all,* he said, his face so close to mine that I could feel his breath on my face. I could smell it, too – the sour smell of cigarettes.

Just fuckin' watch it, that's all.

I turned my head to one side so that I wasn't looking at him. I was determined to continue to ignore him, to put up with whatever he did to me. I still believed that my will was stronger than his, that he would be worn down before I was. But I also knew that ignoring him only provoked him to greater anger and violence. I heard him say: *How's the stomach?* He released me and I braced myself for the blow which duly arrived. He hit me so hard that I was flung backwards, folded up like paper. I wound up sitting on the cold black and white floor tiles. I turned round to spew up the egg sandwich I'd just eaten and found myself on my hands and knees like a sick dog, back arching as I continued to vomit up my food.

When I'd finished retching I sat on the floor again, leaning back against the wall with my knees up close to my chest.

Gilfedder had gone and I hadn't noticed his going nor even what his parting comment might have been. I managed to pull a handkerchief from my pocket and wipe my mouth. I sat there for some minutes and I knew I was completely beaten. The idea that I could somehow wear Gilfedder down seemed laughable. What was I trying to do? – allow myself to be punched so often that eventually he broke his knuckles? My plan was ridiculous, farcical. My stomach ached. I stayed sitting on the floor inhaling from my clothes the smell of herring and puked-up egg sandwiches. I decided that I would get up, clean up the mess in the corridor and go home. After all, what did it matter? I was placing Gilfedder at the centre of my life, moulding my life round my fixation with him. Why continue to do this? I could just walk away. There were other jobs; there were lots of other jobs. I got to my feet. It was difficult to straighten up properly and I leaned against the wall for support. My stomach would hurt for a couple of days, maybe more, but then it would wear off and I wouldn't be here anyway. I would be somewhere else, no longer interested in Gilfedder or herring or working twelve hour shifts in a huge shed full of cold air.

I found a mop and bucket and was just finishing cleaning up the mess when the Mule arrived. *What's up wi' you then?* he asked.

Nothing, I said.

Nothing? He looked at me. *Morgan sent me.*

Did he?

Aye. It was Gilfedder said something to him.

Did he now. And what did he say?

Said you were sick or something.

Well, I was.

Were you?

Something in the sandwich.

Your piece?

Yes.

The Mule took hold of the mop and stopped me from finishing my task. *Gilfedder thumped you, didn't he?*

No, I said, *he didn't.*

The Mule took the mop and bucket from me. *I'll put these away,* he said. *And don't think you're the only one Gilfedder's thumped in the gut.*

He's never hit you, has he? I asked.

Aye, once, the bastard. But he'll no do it again. Reckons

I'm too old, I imagine.

I stepped up to the Mule and took hold of the handle of the mop, partly to steady myself, partly to get close. *You're kidding,* I said. *He hit you? He actually hit you?*

Just the once. As I say, a while ago now.

God almighty, I said. *And you're apologising for him, too. Jesus Christ, I don't believe it.*

He's a sly one, the Mule went on. *Aye, he's thumped one or two of us but there's never any witnesses, like. If he gets you on your own there's no much you can do… I mean, either to prevent it or to do anything about it later.*

Jesus, I said. *Jesus Christ.*

I stepped away, leaned against the wall. I looked at the Mule and wondered if that would be me in thirty years' time.

The Mule said: *Are you going home then?*

No, I said, *I'm not.*

It'll likely get worse.

Likely it will, I said.

We went back to the loading bay. The men were nearly half-way through the next lorry. The first full pallet was being driven off to the freezing room. A thin fog, made up of the men's breath and the vapour rising from the ice packed in the fish boxes, enclosed the men. It spread from the loading bay itself out over the open back of the lorry where Bob and Morrison were still working, shifting crates to the lorry's edge.

Morgan looked at me as I approached. *You OK?* he asked.

Fine, I said. *Fucking sandwich came back on me.* I looked inside the nearest fish box. *What's this? Mackerel?*

Aye, mackerel, Morgan said. *We get them occasionally. Fat little buggers. Have to push them down hard between the slats.*

Yeah?

Yeah. Don't know why we bother.

Right, I said. *Anyway, I'd better get on. I'll take a turn with Gilfedder.*

You'll what?

But I was already away, walking over to where Gilfedder was working, as usual, alone. He didn't notice me as I came up to him.

Come on, Gilfedder, let me give you a hand there, I said.

He turned to look at me. For a moment he was surprised, then he laughed. *You?* he said. *You give me a hand? You're joking.*

No, I said, sounding as breezy as I could manage. *I'd like to give you a hand tonight.*

Well you can just fuck off. He grabbed another crate from the lorry and swung it down onto the pallet.

No, no. Look, I said. *You've just come back after cracking a rib. I mean, you should take it easy, that's all.*

He already had the next crate in his hands, the heavy red gloves tight round the wet wooden handles. He stopped in mid-swing and looked hard at me. Instead of putting the crate onto the pallet he threw it down at his feet on the stone floor of the loading bay. The impact made the contents recoil upwards. Some of the ice spilled out and one mackerel slipped from the box and fell down between the lorry and the edge of the loading bay.

What the fuck are you talking about?

Everybody stopped work and watched us. I spoke confidently, loudly, so that they could all hear. *I'm just saying,* I said, *that you should let someone help you when you're maybe not quite up to it.*

Not up to it? He looked at me first in bewilderment and then in anger. *Not up to it?* He stepped over the fish box he had just flung down and screamed *Fuck off!* at me. He lunged forward and pushed me back, the heels of his hands thumping into my chest. I lost my balance and fell down, clattering into the half-built pallet behind me. But I scrambled back up again as quickly as I could. Morgan, hovering somewhere to my right, was saying: *Now hold on, Donnie, just hold on...* But neither he nor anyone else came near us.

I stepped back up to Gilfedder and said: *But you don't understand, do you? You're a sick man, Gilfedder. You need help. You can't manage on your own.*

I turned away just enough to reduce the full power of the punch. I wanted a bruise, not a broken jaw. But nothing could have prepared me for the explosion of force on the side of my head. It was as if someone had hit me with a fence post. Perhaps only a few seconds passed before I became aware that I was lying on my right side on the floor. My right arm was flung out above my head along the cold wet stone. I could feel dampness seeping through my clothes and reaching my skin. There was a great deal of noise, lots of shouting and running around, it seemed. I could see, before my face, some ice and a couple of mackerel, the deep blue-green sheen on their backs, the thin points of their tails, and I found myself thinking about how big they were, huge in fact, and Morgan was right when he said they wouldn't fit between the freezing plates in the vats. I lay there for some time or perhaps only a few seconds. My face slowly tilted to the floor and my nose became wet. Then I tasted stone and water and fishblood and the oil from the mackerel that scummed the surface of the shallow puddles and invaded the crushed ice that had been scattered across the floor of the loading bay.

Hugh McMillan   *2002*

A GUIDE TO DUMFRIES

That's the Nith,
and that's a herring gull.
There's a man asleep on a bench
beside a herring gull.
There are two alkies
and a herring gull,
isn't that nice?
Now that's a black headed –
no sorry, there was a chip bag in the way –
it's a herring gull.
There's the open top bus tour
with Michael Sullivan showing his arse off the back,
over there by the kebab shop
and those herring gulls.
And here's some drunk Geordies throwing
beer cans at the swan,
because the herring gulls are too fast.
Do you know herring gulls
can hang on thermals
high enough to lose sight of the slack faces,
the boarded up shop fronts,
and garlands of sick,
and see just a patchwork of water,
earth and stone,
the original plan?
Herring gulls can *do* that.
They're a menace.

Valerie Thornton   *2002*

IF ONLY COLL WERE TWO FLOORS DOWN

If only Coll
were two floors down
I could drive (for two hours)
to the Oban
of my front door,
sail down two flights
on the Lord of the Isles
(for three hours)
and walk on the machair
of the back court (for ever)
to the best beach
in the world.

The song of the seal
on the rocks over there
is drowned out
by the sirens
rising and falling
from stone streets.
The slow thunder
of wheely binmen
ebbs and flows
and the smell
of rotting oranges
eclipses acres of clover.

The thrumming
of Archie's lobster boat
is lost in the drum
of a washing machine,
a neighbour
repairing his window
hammers out
the wingbeat of a raven
and, though the rhythm
is right, that phone
will never master
the corncrake's croak.

But you are here
on the southern beach
of this island of city
where later
in the cool of evening
we'll bathe
sleek as seals
in our waves
and whisper softer
than the raven's wing
to charm the short night
slow and long.

BIOGRAPHIES

Dòmhnall Alasdair (Donald Macdonald) was born in Lewis in 1919. He served in the RAF during WW2 and then worked as a teacher of the blind in the Western Isles. He published a collection of poetry, *Bàrdachd Dhòmhnaill Alasdair*, and one of short stories, *Sgeulachdan Dhòmhnaill Alasdair*. He died in 2003.

Meg Bateman was born in Edinburgh in 1959 and learnt Gaelic at university in Aberdeen and in S. Uist. Her collection *Aotromachd/ Lightness* (1997) won an Arts Council award and was shortlisted for the Stakis Prize. She taught at Aberdeen University till 1998 and now works at Sabhal Mòr Ostaig in Skye where she lives with her son.

Margaret Beveridge was born in Kirkintilloch and now lives in Edinburgh where she is a community and adult educator. *Speedy Delivery – Verbal Estimate* was her first published piece of fiction.

Moira Burgess is a novelist, short story writer and literary historian who lives in Glasgow. She is currently busy with some fiction projects and completing a PhD thesis at Glasgow University on supernatural and mythical elements in the work of Naomi Mitchison.

Ron Butlin is an award-winning poet and novelist. His collection of stories, *Vivaldi and the Number 3*, was published this year. Next spring sees the publication of *Without a Backward Glance: New and Selected Poems*, and *No More Angels*. At present he is 'Poet in Residence' at the National Gallery of Scotland.

Gerry Cambridge, born of Irish parents in 1959, is a poet, essayist, and editor of the Scottish-American poetry magazine *The Dark Horse*. His latest collection, *Madame Fi Fi's Farewell and Other Poems* (Luath), appeared in February 2004. He also plays harmonica as part of a duo with Neil MacDonald Thomson, who has put a number of Cambridge's poems to music as an ongoing project and performs them at venues across Scotland.

Marianne Carey was born in 1962 in Glasgow, where she still lives, with her husband and three children. She continues to write – mainly drama – particularly for radio.

Jim Carruth lives in Renfrewshire and is an active member of the Johnstone Writers Group. His work has been widely published in various UK anthologies and magazines. He is currently looking for a publisher for his first collection.

Stewart Conn was born in Glasgow and grew up in Ayrshire. Long resident in Edinburgh, he is currently the capital's poet laureate. His recent publications include *Distances* (Scottish Cultural Press) and *Stolen Light: Selected Poems* published by Bloodaxe Books, from whom *Ghosts at Cockcrow* is forthcoming.

Robert Crawford was born in 1959. Collections of poems include *Assembly* (1990), *Talkies* (1992), *Masculinity* (1996), *Spirit Machines* (1999) and *The Tip of My Tongue* (2003). Lives and works in St Andrews.

David Cunningham was born in Ayrshire. He has worked mainly as a bookseller and educations administrator, and has had short stories published in various magazines and anthologies. He wrote his first novel after many failed attempts to break into Scottish journalism. It is entitled *Cloud World* and is forthcoming from Faber & Faber.

Criosaidh Dick is a Glasgow Highlander. Gaelic is her mother tongue. She started school as a monoglot Gaelic speaker but soon learned to speak Glaswegian and English. Motivation is a great teacher. She studied at Glasgow University, taught at Strathclyde and now farms with her husband and son on the banks of Loch Lomond.

Anne Donovan: winner of the Macallan/Scotland on Sunday Short Story Award in 1997, Anne Donovan is the author of the novel *Buddha Da* and the short story collection, *Hieroglyphics* (both Canongate). *Buddha Da* was short-listed for the Orange Prize, the Whitbread First Novel Award and the Scottish Book of the Year Award, received an SAC Award and won Le Prince Maurice Award in Mauritius.

G.F. Dutton was born in 1924 of Anglo-Scottish parentage has subsequently, when not gracing intercontinental circuses of bio-medical research, lived among Scottish rocks, tenements and weather whose passionate austerities inform four award-winning books of poetry and maybe a spectrum of not-unrelated international publications, scientific or otherwise. He explores widely, driven by the Metaphorical Imperative.

Alexander Fenton CBE, Professor Emeritus of Scottish Ethnology, Director of the European Ethnological Research Centre. Brought up in Drumblade and Auchterless, Aberdeenshire; attended the Universities of Aberdeen (MA, Hon D. Litt), Cambridge (BA) and Edinburgh (D. Litt); author of books on Scottish country life, Orkney and Shetland, farm buildings, etc.; and *Craiters*, a volume of short stories in the Auchterless dialect.

Pete Fortune lives in Dumfries. He writes, 'When the words came easily *NWS* was always one of my favoured outlets. Proud to have appeared in seven editions, and moved that this piece appears here. Lately, writing has been interrupted by study. I now work full time in the social work side of Criminal Justice.'

Paul Foy is a native Glaswegian currently living and working as a Cinema Education Officer in Aberdeen. He has several short stories published in anthologies and magazines, and has written sketches for *Only an Excuse?* and *Chewin' the Fat*.

Graham Fulton's published poetry collections include *Humouring the Iron Bar Man, Knights of the Lower Floors* (both Polygon) and *Ritual Soup and other liquids* (Mariscat). A new collection called *Flying Lessons* is finished and two more, *Think Positive* and *Saved Messages*, are in progress and at an advances stage of completion.

Robin Fulton's *Selected Poems* of 1980 was followed by further collections in 1982, 1990, and 2003. Uncollected poems have appeared in a wide variety of magazines and in Swedish, Spanish and German translations. Between 1967 and 1976 he edited *Lines Review* and the associated books. Recent translations include work by Tomas Transtroemer (Sweden), Olav H. Hauge (Norway) and Henrik Nordbrandt (Denmark).

Janice Galloway is the author of seven books: *The Trick Is To Keep Breathing, Foreign Parts, Blood, Where You Find It, pipelines* (with sculptor Anne Bevan), *Clara* and *Rosengarten*. She has one son and lives in Lanarkshire.

William Gilfedder was born and raised in Glasgow, and went to various schools in the city before leaving to start work at 15. He has had various jobs in and around Glasgow, and has had numerous poems published in several magazines and anthologies.

Valerie Gillies is one of the best-known Scottish poets who writes in English and occasionally in Scots. Her publications include *Tweed Journey* (1989), *The Chanter's Tune* (1990), *The Ringing Rock* (1995), *Men and Beasts* (2000), and *The Lightning Tree* (2002).

Jim Glen has had his poetry and short stories published widely since *The Vase* in 1983 (including other editions of *New Writing Scotland*) and several stories have been broadcast on radio, He still works as a secondary school teacher and recently completed a postgraduate MA in History with the Open University.

John Glenday has published two collections of poetry: *The Apple Ghost* (Peterloo Poets 1989) was awarded a Scottish Arts Council Book Award and *Undark* (Peterloo Poets 1995) was a Poetry Book Society Recommendation for that year. Poems have appeared recently in *New British Poetry* (Gray Wolf Press 2004) He was appointed Scottish/Canadian Exchange Fellow for 1990/91, based at the University of Alberta.

Rody Gorman was born in Dublin in 1960 and now lives on Skye. He has published the poetry collections *Fax and Other Poems*; *Cùis-Ghaoil*; *Bealach Garbh*; *Air a' Charbad fo Thalamh/On the Underground* and *Naomhóga na Laoi*. He also has forthcoming collections from diehard (*Taaaaaaad-haaaaaaal!*) and from Lapwing (*Tóithín ag Tláithínteacht*) in 2004. He is editor of the poetry magazine *An Guth* and has translated many poets' works into Gaelic. His English translations include the poetry of Sorley MacLean.

Andrew Greig was born in 1951 and grew up in Anstruther. His first book of poetry, *White Boats* (with Catherine Lucy Czwerkawska), was published in 1973. His first novel, *Electric Brae* (1992), was shortlisted for the Scottish Writer of the Year award. *The Return of John McNab* (1996) was shortlisted for the Romantic Novelists' Association Award. His most recent books are a collection of poetry, *Into You* (2001), and a fifth novel, *In Another Light* (2004).

Jane Harris's short stories have appeared in a wide variety of anthologies and literary magazines. Her first novel, *The Observations*, will be published by Faber and Faber in spring 2006.

John Herdman was born in Edinburgh in 1941 and now lives in Perthshire. He is a novelist, short story writer and critic whose most recent books of fiction are *Imelda and Other Stories* (1993), *Ghostwriting* (1996) and *The Sinister Cabaret* (2001). He is currently co-editor of *Fras*.

Brent Hodgson has had poetry and fiction published in literary magazines and anthologies. Four pamphlets of his work have been published by independent presses. Two of these pamphlets featured his poetry written in a language that bore a passing resemblance to Medieval Scots.

A.L. Kennedy was born in the North East of Scotland. She has written four collections of short fiction and three novels, two books of non-fiction and a variety of journalism, including a column for *The Guardian*. She has won a number of literary prizes. She also writes for the stage, radio, film and TV. She has sold brushes door-to-door, but currently lectures part-time in the Creative Writing programme at St Andrew's University School of English. In 1993, she was listed among Granta's Best of Young British Novelists. In 2003 she was listed again.

David Kinloch was born in Glasgow in 1959, and is a poet, literary analyst, and academic. Currently a senior lecturer in the Department of English Studies at Strathclyde University, his published collections include *Dustie-Fute*, *Paris-Forfar* and *Un Tour d'Ecosse*. He has also recently received a Robert Louis Stevenson Memorial Award.

Norman Kreitman is a retired research psychiatrist living in Edinburgh, who has written on the theory of metaphor as well as having published three books of poetry (*Touching Rock, Against Leviathan* and *Casanova's 72nd Birthday*). Many other interests but is happiest when fishing.

Douglas Lipton was born and educated in Glasgow. He has lived and worked in Dumfriesshire since the late 1970s. Publications include *The Stone Sleeping-Bag* (Mariscat) and chapbook collections *The Outside World, Fairy Tales* and *Hale-Bopp Poems* (Markings). Douglas Lipton is married with two children. Further information on **www.douglaslipton.co.uk**.

Gerry Loose: poet, editor and artist, whose work may be found inscribed in gardens or printed on the page. Formerly Writer in Residence, Castlemilk; Poet in Residence, Glasgow Botanic Gardens; and Poet in Residence, Jardin des Plantes, Montpelier. Publications include: *Knockariddera, Elementary Particles, a measure, Eitgal, The Botanical Basho*. Currently Creative Director, Peace Garden, Glasgow.

Brian McCabe was born in a small mining community near Edinburgh. He studied Philosophy and English Literature at Edinburgh University. He has lived as a freelance writer since 1980. He has held various writing fellowships, most recently as Writer in Residence for Perth and Kinross Council, based in the William Soutar House in Perth. He lives with his family in Edinburgh. He has published three collections of poetry, the most recent being *Body Parts* (Canongate). He also writes fiction and his most recent collection of short stories *A Date With My Wife* was published by Canongate in June 2001. His *Selected Stories* was published by Argyll in 2003.

Norman MacCaig (1910-1996), born Edinburgh, poet and teacher. He was one of the most distinctive of 20th century Scottish poets, a master of lyric, a brilliant and witty observer. He was awarded the Queen's Gold medal for Poetry in 1986. The poem 'Two Nights' subsequently appeared in his *Collected Poems: A New Edition*, published in 1990 by Chatto & Windus. It is reprinted here by kind permission of Random House Group Ltd.

Murdo Stal MacDonald was born in 1969 on the Isle of Lewis. He lives there with his wife Cath and three kids, Daisy, Sam, and Hector. His most recent poems have appeared in *An Guth*, 2003. He hopes to find the Mangroids at the top of The Tower of Power.

James McGonigal (b. 1947) is a teacher and writer in Glasgow. he has published poetry, short stories, translations and literary criticism as well as school development resources, and co-edited several anthologies of Scottish writing, including *New Writing Scotland*. His prize-winning *Passage/An Pasaíste* is forthcoming from Mariscat Press (2004).

David S Mackenzie is from Easter Ross and lives in London. He is the author of *The Truth of Stone* (Mainstream). *Gilfedder* is from a forthcoming novel, *The Interpretations*.

Alastair Mackie (1925-1995) was born in Aberdeen and graduated from Aberdeen University. After wartime service in the Royal navy he served as an English teacher in Stromness, Orkney, and later in Anstruther, Fife. In his leisure time, Mackie was a prolific poet and translator. He is survived by his wife, Bet, and daughters Frances and Kate.

Hugh McMillan is a widely published poet and short story writer. He lives in Penpont near Dumfries.

Aonghas MacNeacail is a poet, scriptwriter, journalist and playwright who was born on the Isle of Skye in 1942.

Kevin MacNeil was born and raised on the Isle of Lewis. He was British Council Writer in Residence at Uppsala University, Sweden (2002-3) and inaugural Iain Crichton Smith Writing Fellow in the Highlands (1999-2002). Books include *Be Wise Be Otherwise* and *Love and Zen in the Outer Hebrides*, which won the prestigious Tivoli Europa Giovani International Poetry Prize. He has performed his English and Gaelic work in many countries and has written for radio, television and film. His next book is a novel, *The Stornoway Way* (Penguin, Spring 2005). **www.kevinmacneil.com**

Iain S. MacPherson was born in Canada in 1965. He came to Scotland in 1996, where he currently lectures at Sabhal Mòr Ostaig, Isle of Skye. He writes poetry and prose in Gaelic, English and French. In addition to writing and lecturing, he freelances for BBC Gaelic, commenting on the Middle-East.

John Maley lives and works in Glasgow. He is the author of *Daddy's Girl*, a Cannes award-winning short film, and *Delilah's*, a collection of stories set in a fictional gay bar (Neil Wilson Publishing, 2002). He recently completed a feature film script, *The Listen*.

Gordon Meade's most recent collection, *A Man at Sea*, was published in 1993 by diehard publishers. Other collections include *Singing Seals* (1991) and *The Scrimshaw Sailor* (1996). He is presently developing a series of poetry workshops aimed at primary school children with social, emotional, educational and behavioural difficulties.

Edwin Morgan: born Glasgow 1920. War service in Middle East, 1940-1946. Taught English at Glasgow University until 1980. Publications include *Collected Poems*, 1990; *New Selected Poems*, 2000; *A.D.*, 2000; *Cathures*, 2002; *Love and a Life*, 2003. Awarded Queen's Gold Medal for Poetry, 2000. Appointed National Poet for Scotland, 2004.

The author or editor of more than a dozen books, **Donnie O'Rourke**, a graduate of the universities of Glasgow and Cambridge, is a film maker, journalist, broadcaster, translator and song writer. He teaches at the Glasgow School of Art and at Pembroke College Cambridge. Recipient of many fellowships, he lives in Glasgow half the year.

Janet Paisley is an award-winning poet, writer, playwright and scriptwriter whose work includes *Reading the Bones, Ye Cannae Win, Alien Crop* (poetry); *Wild Fire, Not For Glory* (fiction); *Straitjackets, Deep Rising, Winding String, Refuge* (plays); and radio, film and TV drama. The single parent of six sons, she lives near Falkirk.

Roland Portchmouth is the author and illustrator of the children's novel *The Creatures of the Carp*, as well as author of several art and educational books, published both in Britain and America. His paintings have been exhibited at the Royal Academy and elsewhere. His poems and stories have been broadcast on BBC radio, many of which have also been published.

Richard Price's publications include the short story collection *A Boy in Summer* (11:9) and the poetry collections *Frosted*, *Melted* (Diehard) and *Lucky Day* (Carcanet). He is Head of Modern British Collections at the British Library.

Ian Rankin is the author of the internationally-popular Inspector Rebus novels. His books have been translated into 23 languages and have won awards in the UK, USA, France, Germany, Denmark, Sweden and Finland. He started life as a poet and short story writer. *Voyeurism* is one of his earliest published pieces and was written while he was a postgraduate at the University of Edinburgh.

James Robertson has written two books of short stories and several poetry collections, and has edited numerous other books. His first novel, *The Fanatic*, was published in 2000. His second, *Joseph Knight*, was published in 2003 and won both the Saltire and Scottish Arts Council Book of the Year awards. He lives in Angus.

Dilys Rose grew up in Glasgow and now lives in Edinburgh where she is currently Writer in Residence at Edinburgh University. She writes mainly fiction and poetry but has recently collaborated with composers and visual artists. Her most recent publications are *Lure* (poetry) and *Once Upon our Time*, new Portrait Miniatures (with Moyna Flannigan and Keith Hartley). A new collection of stories, *Lord of Illusions*, is forthcoming, as is her *Selected Stories*.

One of Scotland's greatest 20th-century writers, **Iain Crichton Smith** was born in Glasgow in 1928, and moved to Lewis two years later. Although a frequent traveller, lecturing, visiting and giving poetry readings around the world, he remained very much a Highland writer, with Gaelic culture, history and landscape informing his work. He lived in the village of Taynuilt, near Oban, with his wife Donalda, until his death in 1998.

Ian Stephen, born Stornoway, 1955. Poetry and short stories from Dangaroo Press; Polygon; Morning Star and pocket-books. Creative Scotland Award. Contributor to *Zenomap* (Venice Biennale 2003). 'It's about this', a poem-log of a voyage for StAnza, Nomad (Survivors Press), 2004. 'Poetry without Borders', Czech Republic, 2004.

Derick S. Thomson – born 1921 in Stornoway, Isle of Lewis. Educated at the Nicolson Institute, then the University of Aberdeen, and Emmanuel College Cambridge. Lecturer in Welsh at Glasgow University, Reader in Celtic at Aberdeen University, Professor of Celtic at Glasgow University (1963-91). Married to Carol Galbraith 1952; five sons, one daughter. Author of many books and articles, including *The Gaelic Sources of Macpherson's* Ossian, *An Introduction to Gaelic Poetry* and *The Companion to Gaelic Scotland*. Author of seven collections of Gaelic poetry, including the Collected Poems *Creachadh ne Clàrsaich / Plundering the Harp*. Editor of *Gairm*, the Gaelic quarterly, 1952-2002.

Valerie Thornton is an award-winning writer of short stories and poetry. She has been short-listed for the Macallan/SoS Prize and both short-listed and a prize-winner in the Asham Prize. She is also an editor and a teacher of creative writing at all educational levels, and has just completed a three-year Royal Literary Fund Fellowship at Glasgow University.

Gael Turnbull who died in July 2004, was a much-loved poet, publisher (Migrant Press and minimal missives), doctor and morris dancer. *A Gathering Of Poems 1950-1980* was published by Anvil Press in 1983. Two publications are in progress: *Dividings* (Mariscat, for December 2004) and a volume of selected poems, *Time is a Fisherman* (Etruscan with Mariscat, for 2005).

Irvine Welsh was born in Leith in 1961 and grew up in Muirhouse, in Edinburgh. Stories and parts of what would later become *Trainspotting* appeared in several publications including *New Writing Scotland* in the early 1990s.

Trainspotting was published in 1993, and has been followed by several other novels, scripts and short-story collections.

Brian Whittingham was born in, and lives in, Glasgow. Poet, playwright, fiction writer, editor, creative writing tutor and lecturer. Partakes of a refreshment in the Waldorf and The Ritz. Recent poetry collections include *Drink the Green Fairy* – Luath Press and *The Old Man from Brooklyn and The Charing Cross Carpet* – Mariscat Press.

Hamish Whyte (born 1947) is a poet, editor, translator and former librarian. He runs Mariscat Press and is an Honorary Research Fellow at the Department of Scottish Literature, Glasgow University. He has edited several anthologies as well as coediting numbers 7-11 and 20-21 of *New Writing Scotland*. He has recently moved from Glasgow to Edinburgh.

Rachel Yule taught English in schools in Lanark, London, Glasgow and Edinburgh, then switched to Further Education. Now retired she is enjoying the activities of Edinburgh Writers' Club, Citadel Arts Group and Broadside (Women Playwrights in Scotland) and earning some pocket money.